Walking through Shadows

Walking through Shadows

Finding Hope in a World of Pain

Carl Wieland · Ken Ham

Master Books

First printing: July 2002
Second printing: March 2003

ISBN: 0-89051-381-3
Library of Congress Catalog Card Number: 2002105386

Bible quotations are mainly from the *New International
Version*, Zondervan, Grand Rapids, MI.

Printed in the United States of America.

Please visit our website for other great titles:
www.masterbooks.net

For information regarding author interviews, please
contact the publicity department at (870) 438-5288.

This book is dedicated to all those members of each of our families that have suffered so much through the events described herein. We want to especially acknowledge the anguish of our dear mothers, as they watched the suffering of those they brought into the world. It is our prayer that millions may read this book and gain salvation and comfort in a dying world.

Contents

Foreword

Why do righteous people suffer? Why do the worst things sometimes happen to the best of people? Those questions go to the heart of one of the most difficult and most persistent of all metaphysical problems.

It is also one of the oldest dilemmas facing the human race. The Book of Job — probably the earliest book in the Old Testament canon — was written to explore those very questions. Job's experience not only gives us a window into the workings of the spirit world; it also reminds us that even in the midst of our sufferings, God is worthy of our praise. In fact, suffering properly viewed is a reason to praise God, not to doubt Him. In the end, God reminds Job that as Creator and Lord of all, He is utterly sovereign and has every right to do whatever He chooses without needing to justify himself to anyone. He isn't obligated to answer all the questions we raise. He doesn't owe us any explanations.

And yet God *has* graciously given us much in the way of revealed truth and precious promises that can help us understand and endure our sufferings. Consider, for example, what God has told us about himself: He is good. He is pure light in whom there is no darkness at all. He is worthy of our absolute trust and loyalty. He is gracious and full of tender mercy. He sovereignly controls everything that happens, so that no matter how chaotic and turbulent the circumstances of life may *seem,* we're not to think God has lost control. He limits our temptations to no more than we can endure, and He provides a way of escape from all evil enticements. He gives us grace to endure the trials of life, and strength and comfort to withstand the pain of suffering. He never changes, never wavers, never slumbers or sleeps — and never lets even the tiniest sparrow out of His sight. Best of all, He promises to make all things work together for the ultimate good of those who love Him.

All those things are germane to the problem of suffering. Anyone who genuinely believes those truths and trusts those promises ought to find them *sufficient* even if not completely satisfying to our intellectual curiosity.

But sometimes our trials are so grievous, and evil circumstances seem so oppressive, that our emotions overwhelm our minds, and what we *feel* dominates and threatens to overcome what we *know.* Every thoughtful person at one time or another will still long for a better understanding or a more thorough explanation of why God allows so much suffering. That is especially true in this era of war, suicide bombings, and terrorist attacks.

Ken Ham and Carl Wieland have written this book to address these difficult issues. They write with passion and empathy, as only those who know suffering firsthand can do. They also write with sound biblical insight, allowing the clear light of Scripture to illuminate the dark corners of the problem of suffering.

Scripture says one of the reasons God allows us to suffer is so that He can comfort us and thus equip us to comfort others in their suffering (2 Cor. 1:3-4). Ken and Carl have found rich consolation from the heart of God in their own sufferings, and one of the beautiful fruits of that suffering is this book. Many will find it a rich source of comfort and encouragement in the midst of their trials. Others will find biblical help for questions that may have long troubled them. All will be reminded of the goodness of God to His people and His precious promise that the sufferings of this present time are not even worthy to be compared with the glory that will be revealed in us throughout all eternity.

John MacArthur
Pastor, Grace Community Church
Sun Valley, California

Part One

CALAMITY IN THE OUTBACK

Carl Wieland

Chapter 1

Life's Sudden U-turn

"Plastic surgeons can do wonderful things these days." Biting her trembling lower lip as she held the mirror in front of me, my mother was fighting back the tears as she spoke. The grotesque visage within the frame slowly came into focus; that was supposed to be me, but I couldn't recognize "me." One-half of this misshapen countenance was facing me, the other half staring off askew in another direction altogether. The glazed, sunken eye belonging to that disconnected half was sitting at a different level to the other eye. Instead of a nose, this alien face had a narrow, flat sliver of skin, with one "nostril" opening at its base.

Nearly all the facial contours that make us each recognizably unique — cheekbones and the like — had been smashed and distorted by massive impact. My nose had been largely torn off. Despite my medical training, I was not in a frame of mind for dispassionate analysis of my injuries. A numb horror fought for dominance with the infused narcotic medication clouding my consciousness. I couldn't speak because of the tracheotomy tube entering my throat. All I could weakly scrawl on the piece of paper in front of me was, "Looks like the man from Mars." I sank back into the bed of the hospital I would inhabit for the next half-year or so.

The painkilling drugs were not the only thing making me mercifully hazy — I had not long emerged from several days of unconsciousness in intensive care. I was only gradually beginning to piece together, from what my family was telling me, what had happened to put me here.

For some 13 years I had been a family doctor. Now, at the age of 36, I had suddenly become an avid consumer, instead of a provider, of medical care. All the result of a split-second highway impact in which my four-wheel-drive vehicle had collided with a fully-laden fuel tanker at a combined impact speed of 110 mph (180 kph).

My wife had a serious medical condition at the time, which seemed to be partially relieved in steamy tropical weather. To help relieve, even if only a little, this distressingly painful syndrome, we had decided to move to Cairns, in Australia's tropical far north, to "start over." Our house and my practice in South Australia's capital, Adelaide, had sold readily. We had already bought a house in Cairns and sent our furniture on ahead. Little did we know that it would take over six months before we would "catch up" with our possessions again.

The plan was that we would take our two cars up to Cairns via the central Australian outback. For the first leg, about 900 miles (1400 km), we would travel on the famous Ghan train, which took cars as well, to Alice Springs. We really looked forward to driving the remaining 1,500 miles (2400 km), especially the first part in the remote Northern Territory. We knew and loved the lonely outback highways;

the vast desert flatness stretching to the horizon, hour after hour with seldom a vehicle; the brilliant reddish-purple desert dawns silhouetting scraggly excuses for trees; the occasional eagle looking up from its feast of road-kill kangaroo.

It was a sunny day in May 1986 when we unloaded our cars from the train in "Alice," as Australians call their famous Red Centre town. We were feeling really upbeat, thanking God for being alive. I would lead the way in our 4WD diesel-powered Holden Jackaroo (a rebadged Isuzu Trooper) with our 11-year-old daughter Lisa in the front. My wife would follow in our small sedan, accompanied by our 14-year-old daughter Lara. The Northern Territory, the closest thing to an unspoilt "frontier" state in this wonderful country, had no speed limits. Normally I would have wanted to cruise that long, straight traffic-sparse highway as fast as the Jackaroo would want to go. But I thought that this time, being in convoy, I would use the vehicle's hand throttle to keep its speed constant at a relatively staid 70 mph (110 kph).

The first hour or so rolled by, mile after mile of highway with nothing but flat sandy desert on either side, as far as the eye could see. It was the early afternoon, and my neck was aching a little from an old whiplash injury. Lisa was whiling away the time with some toys on her lap. I asked her to put a pillow behind my neck, and half-jokingly told her to wake me up if I started to seem drowsy.

The rest of my family, in the car behind me, saw the

The wrecked vehicle in an Alice Springs salvage yard, in the same position as after the accident, resting on the driver's side. The roof is still peeled back where it was cut open to extract the driver, several hours after the impact.

whole horror. A large fuel tanker was coming the other way, in contrast to this road's normal loneliness, at 45 mph (70 kph). They saw the Jackaroo drift directly into its path. The police later told them that I must have fallen momentarily asleep. Had I nodded off a split second before or after, there would have been nothing to collide with. No other vehicles for miles in either direction. No ditches, no utility poles, no trees to speak of.

The fuel tanker driver, I was told later, tried to swerve out of the way, but the Jackaroo hurtled headlong into the massive vehicle, just off center. The tanker rolled over three times. The tanker had a huge weight advantage, and its driver, who was walking around immediately afterwards, apparently only suffered minor injury. My vehicle flipped on its side, then spun around. In a split second, the one-year-old

The underneath shows the solid chassis members of this small truck buckled under the force of collision with the much heavier vehicle, at a combined speed of 110 mph (180 kph).

The interior of the driver's compartment

car had been converted into about $200 worth of scrap. Almost all trucks on Aus-tralia's major highways are fitted with large "bull bars" to deflect pass-ing "roos" and avoid damage, even when impacting stray cattle. The Jack-aroo had one of these too, a massive steel construction that was now twisted back to be, on the driver's side, only about three inches from the windshield. Photos afterward also showed that the vehicle's solid steel chassis members had buckled into "z" shapes from absorbing so much of the thunderous impact.

With all that grinding, sparking metal and thousands of gallons of fuel sloshing over the road around the car, instant incineration seemed natural to expect. Mercifully, though, both vehicles were diesel-powered — and the fuel carried by the tanker was diesel, too, which doesn't ignite readily.

Mercy in the Midst of Disaster

With the wreck lying on its side, Lisa's passenger seat was now on top. After the side window above her frightened face, surrounded by a cocoon of mangled metal, was smashed, she was extricated to her mother's arms. Incredibly, she had suffered only some minor bruising and a scratch on her knee. Apparently, I remained conscious for a half hour or so. Peering inside the wreckage, the family could see a mangled, bloodstained face, its portions sliding around as I tried to speak, nose hanging by a shred, right eye dangling several inches below its normal position. Though I don't recall the impact, I recall portions of those first few minutes, and I didn't feel any pain in my face. The blinding, searing pain from my right thigh overwhelmed everything else. I remember saying, "Get the jack, lift the car off my leg." Weeks later I found out that the pain was because the jagged end of my snapped right thighbone had torn its way through the flesh to the outside.

I recall hearing some voices and me weakly urging them to "get the bag ... pethidine ... injection." Earlier that day, as we had been taking the cars off the train, for some reason I had taken my "doctor's bag" with its store of emergency medications from the roomy Jackaroo and stuffed it into the already overloaded four-cylinder Ford sedan. Humanly speaking, it made no sense. But if I hadn't, the bag with its store of narcotic painkilling injections would have been, if not destroyed, inaccessible. As it was, I could now have something that would dull the worst of the pain, and lessen the shock, injected into whatever portion of me they could get to through the mangled metal.

The real agony was for those loved ones outside, watching helplessly, with no car in sight. Eventually, after over an hour of what must have been the most exquisite mental torture for them, a tour bus arrived on the scene. The bus used its powerful on-board radio to contact the authorities in Alice, 89 miles (143 km) south. A retired doctor passenger managed to find the fading, bounding pulse on my long-since-unconscious body. His idea of "comfort" consisted in telling my distraught wife she should prepare herself for the fact that I would not survive. That, and forcing slugs of whiskey down her reluctant throat.

In retrospect, my survival was unlikely, medically speaking. Besides the shattered face, there was the substantial blood loss from the severed right leg bone lacerating its way through the front of the thigh muscle to the outside. My family was unable to reach this major wound in order to staunch it. The force of the impact driving my legs into my upper body had fractured both hip sockets. In my lower right leg, both bones were broken, too, as was the left splint bone. The right kneecap was shattered, some of its pieces visible through a gaping hole over it. Then there were five broken ribs, a crushed chest and a collapsed lung due to what is called a pneumothorax (air in the chest cavity), not to mention multiple surface lacerations.

Ironically, when I had bought the car, I had paid extra for the option of having a laminated windshield. This was supposed to be safer; instead of shattering into a zillion pieces, when broken, it would only shatter along a few lines, making it easier for the driver to keep seeing through. Unfortunately, it meant in my case that it broke into several dagger-like pieces. One of these pierced my right eye, carefully carving out most of the iris. A friend traveling past the site a few weeks later found the sunglasses I had been wearing. The right plastic lens had a central hole surrounded by bloodstaining, where the glass "dagger" had neatly done its work before withdrawing again.

Incidentally, a policeman from Alice Springs told me later that the wreck of the tanker, beyond salvage so far into the outback, had simply been buried. "They dug a big trench with a dozer and just pushed it in and covered it up." One would think it would have been the passengers of the Jackaroo they buried, not the big truck.

Chapter 2

Making Sense of It All

In the months and years after this accident, I was intrigued to hear a number of my Christian acquaintances speaking as if somehow God had been "caught napping" by my accident. From the moment I had opened my practice, I had deliberately not worked full-time, so I could be involved in part-time ministry, defending and proclaiming the truth and authority of the Bible in the areas of creation versus evolution, Bible/science issues and so on. I was involved in supporting, both financially and through giving lectures on its behalf, the ministry that had been set up in Queensland by Ken Ham and others, later to become *Answers in Genesis*. The magazine I had commenced in my home was beginning, via that Queensland-based ministry, its worldwide outreach (*Creation* magazine, now going to over 120 countries). So it was natural for my acquaintances to see the whole thing in terms of Satan trying to destroy this ongoing work. But it was as if they saw this attack of the enemy as having occurred behind God's back, that it was somehow "just as well God acted in time" to prevent worse injury.

However, as I would have said long before the incident, the God of the Bible, Creator of heaven and earth, is ultimately sovereign over all, and nothing catches Him by surprise. In fact, in a sense (as others have pointed out), "even the devil works for God." Satan can do nothing to us without God's permission — check out Job 1:1–12, also Luke 22:31–32. When the evil one sought to manipulate human events to nail Christ to that cross, all of this was foreknown and a part of God's eternal plan. So, too, when "bad things" happen to us, we need to understand that they are not without plan and purpose in the mind of God — whether we can see that plan or not at the time, or indeed ever during our lifetime.

Why Me?

Ironically, I had on a number of occasions given sermons on this whole issue of "Death and Suffering." In them, I had talked about the common Christian reaction to suffering, namely to ask, "Why me?" which of course seldom reflects abstract philosophical curiosity, but is more of a shorthand for "What have I done to deserve this?"

In these talks, I would naturally make the usual point concerning Job's friends, the people killed by the fall of the tower of Siloam in Luke chapter 13, and the man born blind in John chapter 9 — namely that individual calamity is not necessarily the result of individual sin. The writer of Psalm 73 cried out to God concerning the apparent "disconnect" between what happens to a person in this life and whatever good or evil they have done, as he saw the wicked prosper.

But the question "Why me?" when asked by a suffering Christian, usually goes deeper than a puzzling over what sin one must have committed. It usually carries a component of resentment, namely a demand to know how our lives could possibly have been bad enough to deserve this. Almost as in, "How dare God do this to *me*? Haven't I become a child of His? He's supposed to look after me."

I recall making the point, in these pre-accident sermons, that a more logical and appropriate thing to ask was really, "Why *not* me?" Why should I (or you) be more special than that Ethiopian Christian, starving slowly to death while crying out to God? Or more special than the apostle Paul, who was repeatedly whipped, imprisoned, and finally executed? Or those Christians torn apart by Nero's lions?

Much of this "Why me?" resentment in the face of suffering is due to our increasingly me-centered age, I would point out to congregations. The dominance of evolutionary thinking has led to a watering-down of the authority of the Bible in general, accompanied by a dulling to the awful reality of sin. We tend to see sin in relation to how it affects *us*, rather than its awesome affront to a holy, sovereign God.

In addition to the resentment, there is also a genuine, puzzling lack of understanding of this whole issue of suffering. Because Christians have tended to ignore the reality of Genesis history ("it's too controversial") they have also pushed aside the biblical Curse in their thinking. But it is that Curse on creation, due to sin, that is the ultimate reason why all of us, Christian and non-Christian alike, still age (very often accompanied by sickness), and eventually *all* die.[1] If we were still living in an unfallen world, there would be no possibility of disease or accident blighting our

---

1 The only historically recorded exceptions, both clearly the result of miraculous intervention, were Enoch and Elijah in the Old Testament. And, of course, those who are alive at the time of Christ's return will also not taste death.

lives. So the answer to the question of "why bad things happen" is tied up with the fact that we live in a cursed, fallen world. This is due to sin in a general sense, though not a direct consequence of any particular individual sin we may have committed, I would say.

Since my conversion, I have never ceased to be amazed at how few Christians really view reality centered around the "big picture" of biblical history. I find that it makes a tremendous difference to our approach to everything that matters. The biblical grand sweep is from the creation of a truly good world (Gen. 1:31), a Fall which affected the whole universe (Gen. 3), now groaning in bondage to decay (Rom. 8:19–22), through Calvary's redemption to the still-future restoration of a sinless, deathless condition in the new heaven and new earth, following removal of the Genesis curse (Rev. 22:3). Focused on this, it becomes much easier to keep our perspective centered on God.

From that vantage point, I would say in such sermons, we will find it much harder to bemoan our lot or angrily demand to know why God would dare do this to us. We will more readily see that we do well to join Job in falling down in dust and ashes before Him (Job 42:6). We should be in awe of God's amazing, undeserved mercy in having chosen us in Christ before the world began (Eph. 1:4). None of us deserve anything less, from God's perspective, than the worst we can imagine. And in all situations, I would say, there is always something left to be thankful for. The peace of God which passes all understanding (Phil. 4:7) is conditional upon such thankfulness (v. 6).

Putting Theory into Practice

Was all of that just theory, some dry theological/academic approach? Was it some unreal sermonizing that went nowhere when faced with the harsh reality of actual, personal suffering? It seemed almost as if God was asking me now whether, having preached on these things, I was able to "put my money where my mouth is," as the saying goes. I can say with a great sense of relief that having tried to gain the appropriate biblical/theological understanding of such matters was not just some theoretical exercise. Having worked through the issues in principle beforehand made an *enormous difference* when the rubber hit the road in my own life.

That does not mean, of course, that there were no tears, that there was no grief, no sense of loss, no anguish. There were lots of all of those along the way. But I can honestly say that throughout my whole ordeal (which included a total of 56 operations over the next seven years), I did not spend a single tortured minute asking "why" or "why me."

Chapter 3

Explaining Those "Bad Things"

As indicated before, the most important aspect in understanding the whole issue of suffering was, for me, the reality of the Genesis curse, and God's sovereign right to have so judged the world. I had been an atheist all the way through university, primarily because I had been led to believe that evolution and millions of years represented the "scientific truth." So there was no need to postulate a Designer to explain all that seeming design out there in the living world. It also meant that the Bible, especially in its opening chapters (Genesis), was demonstrably, palpably, historically untrue. I had read enough of it to realize that the history in Genesis was the very basis for the whole Christian gospel. The "good news" of the gospel of Jesus Christ, the "last Adam" (1 Cor. 15:45) only made sense in the context of the "bad news" concerning the "first Adam."

I had realized in my teens that if Genesis were true, it was easy to understand the "big picture" of why there were "bad things" in a world made by a God of love. The "man's sin-death" axis, the whole notion of creation/Fall/restoration, was woven all the way through the Bible. Death and suffering were, in the Bible, temporary intruders into a once-perfect creation, ones that would be done away with. (Death itself is called "the last enemy" in 1 Corinthians 15:26.) But I had become convinced, through glossy, popular "science" depictions in magazines, that the dead bones in the fossil record, many of which show signs of violence, suffering. and disease, even cancer, had accumulated over millions of years. These "bad things" were therefore in existence long before there could have been anyone called Adam. So the whole idea of the creation of a good world, ruined by sin, was wrong, and there was thus no rational Christian framework within which to answer the question, "Why would a God of love tolerate a world of death and suffering?"

As an atheist challenging Christians on campus, I would point out that if they believed that God used evolution, then He used death and suffering to create. Even those who did not believe in evolution, but accepted geology's long-age system, were telling me that God superintended a world for hundreds of millions of years of watching the strong wipe out the weak, animals rip each other's throats out, and so on. He only got around to making man after an apparent trial and error process with lots of purposeless creations (e.g.. dinosaurs that were wiped out again before any person ever saw them, in that view), calamities, extinctions, and disease along the way. Then, finally, He calls it "all very good"? It made no sense.

Importantly, evolution and/or the millions of years also meant to me that the words of Jesus Christ were mistaken. For example, in Matthew 19:4 and Mark 10:6, Jesus makes it clear that He believes that people were there from the beginning of creation (not billions of years after the beginning, sort of towards the end, as many Christians blithely think it's okay to swallow). The basic Christian claim is that Jesus *is* God, the Creator himself, the second person of the Trinity, who was there from before the beginning of time, and who is the truth. So these things were a death blow to any rational faith. I could see that those who tried to "save" the Bible by disconnecting it from anything to do with the real world ("it's only about faith, morality, relationship with God . . .") were not only kidding themselves, but were helping to undermine their own position. What sense did it make to believe in the Bible's claims about an afterlife if its claims about history were so obviously wrong? As Jesus himself asked rhetorically in John 3:12, what sense did it make to expect His hearers to believe Him about "heavenly" things if they did not believe when He told them about "earthly" things?

This intellectual repudiation of the Bible led, consistently I believe, to my conviction that philosophical materialism had to be correct. Matter was the only reality; there was no supernatural. I could in principle explain everything by the laws of physics and chemistry (given the "known mechanisms of biological evolution"). What about claims of things like ESP, supernatural occurrences, and so on? Well, there was no repeatable laboratory evidence, and our evolved minds were fallible — psychology was the explanation for such fantasies.

But God pursued me, in a fairly dramatic way, to shatter this naively arrogant view. Our family became involved with a man who was a practicing Satanist. We didn't know this (he said he was into "natural religion"), but it wouldn't have worried me, anyway. The rational deduction from evolution/long ages was that the *biblical* God most certainly did not exist, and therefore neither did angels, demons, nor Satan.

Atheism Convincingly Refuted

Strange things began to happen in our family. Without seeking to glorify the occult, let me tell you of just one event which showed me, with mathematical certainty, that my world view could not explain it. A dentistry student friend and myself, for fun, had set up a "mind-reading" stunt using a pack of cards. If I asked him, "Which card am I holding up at the moment?" the question itself constituted a code we had worked out in advance, one which told him what card it was. So for another card, the question would be different; for example, "Can you tell me what card I'm looking at right now?" which would secretly reveal the exact card, and so on. A simple party trick. We demonstrated this to my wife, who was amazed, believing that we could indeed read minds. "Can I try that?" she asked. We looked at each other and winked. "Sure, why not?" I grinned. It would be fun to let her try in vain for a while, and then reveal that she had been duped.

The first card I pulled off the top of the deck just happened to be the ace of spades. Now remember, I was not using the code, because she did not know it, anyway, so what would be the point? Her head was buried in her hands for a long time, and we were about to let her in on the secret, when she said, "Wait, I can see something floating towards me . . . a card. . . ." "Okay, what sort of card?" I asked, cynically. I remembered just then that she had never played cards in her life, and did not know the names of the cards or suits, etc. But she went on and described it as a card bearing the letter "A," with a black object on it, and drew the shape of the spades symbol in the air. I looked at my friend, he looked at me, and

I think we both decided, well, even people who don't play cards have heard of the ace of spades. It was probably buried deep in her unconscious. That was the natural first thing for anyone to guess at — no big deal.

I pulled up the next card for my friend and me to see. There was no one else in the room, and my wife was sitting on the other side, quite a way off. I said, "Okay, how about this one?" Again, she described it correctly. The hair started to rise on the back of my neck, even more so when she got the next eight in succession exactly right. Ten in all, in unbroken succession, from a randomly shuffled deck. Her lack of knowledge of card symbols made even three in a row staggeringly improbable, but let's assume that she *did* know exactly what a deck of cards was. The probability that what we had just seen with our own eyes was a random occurrence was still a mind-popping one chance in 50 million *billion*! A total impossibility.

I could go on about more such occurrences, which became increasingly sinister, and about the specific ways in which my mother and younger sister, who had become Christians by then, were praying when they suspected that our household was under demonic assault. And about the way that their simple, heartfelt, believing prayers, without us knowing what they were, seemed to have an obvious, incredible effect, amounting to something like total "control" over (in the sense of protection) what was going on.

Suffice it to say that no rational person in my situation could go on believing in materialism much longer. What I had seen was aching for an explanation. I had read widely enough to know that the only thing that fitted the facts was that I was witnessing the spiritual warfare between Christ and Satan, just as my mother and sisters believed it. But I had been so sure that they were deluded simpletons, closing their minds to the facts of science. It was almost as if God had taken me by the scruff of the neck and was showing me that my world view was wrong. As I have since quipped, now I had been shown that the "bad guys" were for real, it made good sense for me to join up with the "good guys" as soon as possible.

Problem — those long astronomical and geological ages, and the associated fossils, reared their heads. I wanted to become a Christian, but it all had to make sense, it had to hang together. If Christianity, and particularly the history of all things given in the Bible in "big picture" form, contradicted reality, then its claim to be a revelation from the Maker himself was fatally flawed. I had heard many feeble attempts by Christians to try to weave the millions of years into the Bible, but they had turned me *away* from Christianity. These notions seemed not only highly contrived and "slippery," they glossed over huge, glaring inconsistencies with what the Bible so plainly taught.

Incidentally, all my atheist/humanist acquaintances at the time thought the same. We held such seeming deviousness in contempt. The man who coined the word "agnostic" to describe himself — Thomas Huxley, a.k.a. "Darwin's Bulldog" — also waxed sarcastic against such similarly convenient flexibility of belief in his day. Today, prominent humanists and atheists have not changed their minds about the inconsistency of people who hold to Christianity and at the same time hold to evolution/long ages. But in their stand against "fundamentalism" (a new term of abuse), particularly creationism, they will openly side with those who compromise and distort what the Bible teaches.

Lenin is said to have invented the term "useful idiots" for those pro-Communist sympathizers in the West whom he similarly despised — for foolishly undermining their own foundation — but used.

My other, older sister, who now lived a long way away, was the first of the family to have become a Christian, many years previously, at age 14. I will be forever grateful that right at that time she sent me a copy of Morris and Whitcomb's classic creationist book *The Genesis Flood*. Though now outdated in some areas, it let me see then that the issue was not so much about the facts of science but about how they were interpreted. If you started with the Bible, the same facts made a great deal of sense in a young-world, catastrophic framework. This did not imply that one would have all the answers or that all problems would be magically solved. I knew that science was all about continually solving ongoing problems and changing older ideas in the light of new information.

It was as if the scales fell from my eyes. Shortly afterward, I bowed the knee to Jesus Christ in belief for the forgiveness of my sin, my life of rebellion against Him. So it was no surprise that I would be burdened to share this incredibly powerful way of thinking with people everywhere. I wanted to ensure that God-honoring creation materials got into as many hands as possible. I particularly wanted to see good glossy periodicals to counter the ones that had so blinded me — hence my passion for what became *Creation* magazine. (Incidentally, once we had become Christians, all of the strange "gifts" and occurrences stopped instantly.)

Well, all of that was a long background to the way in which a thoroughly biblical world view, especially concerning death and suffering, made an enormous difference to me in my time of trial. Particularly the knowledge of the Curse. No matter what temporary ways we find to alleviate its effects, ultimately we all remain under the Curse and we all succumb to it. Like flowers, we blossom for a while, then our physical bodies wither as grass, returning to the dust (raw materials) from which we were constructed in the first place (Job 14:1–2; Gen. 3:19).[1]

---

1 Our first ancestor, Adam, was assembled directly from the dust, but each of us is also assembled from simple raw materials, under the direction of the programmed instructions in our biological machinery. This programming (information) was initially imposed on raw matter by God, then passed on from our first parents via the marvelously designed mechanisms of inheritance, i.e., repeated copying of the information.

Chapter 4

Hey, Be Grateful

The thankfulness in the midst of suffering which I had previously only preached about became a very important principle for me. Even in the darkest moments (and there were many), I could always find something for which to be immensely thankful to my Lord and Savior. For one thing, my little daughter's mind-bogglingly wonderful escape from serious injury in the same crash. How much harder it would have been for me, lifelong, had she been killed or, worse yet, maimed for life. She is now the mother of three wonderful children. The Bible tells us to give thanks in all things, thinking on those things that are true, pure, honest, just, and lovely (1 Thess. 5:18; Phil. 4:8). Well, if ever there was a beautiful thing to thank and praise God for, in addition to who He was, and what He did for me on the Cross for all eternity, that was it, I felt, as I clung to this among many comforts.

And there were indeed many indications of mercy in the midst of catastrophe. The hours I spent in the wreck, with the immense loss of blood, should have been fatal for me. But as it turned out, only two weeks before, the Northern Territory government had decided to install an emergency nurse station at a remote outpost called Ti-Tree, 50 miles (80 km) away from the accident site. The nurse who had arrived on the scene as soon as she could tried hard to find an entry into my collapsed neck veins. It must have been immensely difficult considering the small amount of access permitted by the wreckage. But eventually she was able to get a line in, and the plasma expander that was set dripping into my bloodstream was one more difference-maker between life and death. I was told later that my 14-year-old daughter was given the job of holding the plasma bottle up so that gravity could do its job. Lara is now a highly qualified rural Christian doctor with Australia's famous Royal Flying Doctor Service, her life mostly spent serving on remote Aboriginal communities in the Gulf of Carpentaria. She stood there motionless, hour after hour, holding the bottle which offered hope for her father's life, while tears flowed silently down her cheeks.

Another incredible blessing concerned the "jaws of life," the well-known device used to extricate people trapped in wrecked vehicles. In densely populated parts of the Western world, the availability of such technology is taken for granted, as it is in most parts of Australia. But the Northern Territory covers an area bigger than France, Spain, and Italy combined. At that time, it contained only about 150,000 people. Most of them were in the two main population centers — Alice Springs, and the bigger one by far, the capital Darwin, some 950 miles (1500 km) to the north of Alice. The Territory government had decided it could only afford one such gadget. The logical place for it to spend its time was in Darwin, where most of the people and traffic were. As it happened, it was in Alice that day, which meant that it could be brought to this remote scene in time to cut me out before my life ebbed away.

Amazingly, there was also, right at that time, in the faraway outback town of Alice Springs, a national convention of ambulance personnel. So even though the accident was so far away from any of Australia's real cities, the paramedic who attended me turned out to be the country's finest. He apparently very quickly decided that I would not last an ambulance trip. He called in a mining company's helicopter for the trip, without which I would, humanly speaking, probably not have survived.

At the base hospital in Alice, I underwent a preliminary six-hour operation to "patch up" the worst of the injuries. But the facilities in this frontier town were very limited, and my shattered frame, by now long since on a mechanical ventilator, needed more high-tech intervention to stay alive. The nearest metropolitan center that would have the appropriate facilities was Adelaide, the city I had not long left. Accompanied by a specialist anesthetist and a senior nurse, I was put onto a commercial passenger flight for the long journey all the way back down south again.

By now the word had spread to family and friends back in Adelaide, and much prayer was underway. One surgeon friend at the main hospital there, the Royal Adelaide, had had the word passed to him from Alice that I was not likely to arrive alive. There was apparently x-ray evidence of a widening mediastinum (the part between the two lungs occupied by the heart and great vessels) associated with a rapidly dropping blood pressure. That could only mean that there was a ruptured aorta (the main artery leading from the heart) and the blood leaking into this mediastinal area was forcing the lungs apart. This friend organized a prayer chain through the night, focusing on that deadly leak. With 120 air miles still to go to Adelaide, the specialist on board apparently decided that all the massive amount of blood transfusion I had already had was not sufficient if I was going to make it. So the decision was made to stop at Whyalla, a country outpost, to "top up" with more blood. Toward the end of the journey, the plane was not even allowed to land for a while, as the airport was fogbound. The tension for family and friends must have been immense.

But amazingly, at the Royal Adelaide Hospital, the x-ray evidence of mediastinal widening was no longer there. In cautious disbelief, the doctors passed a plastic tube into the artery in my thigh, threading it up to the big artery leading from the heart. Injecting a dye that was opaque to x-rays, they were looking for a leak. But there was none to be found. If a miraculous healing did occur there (and the conclusion is hard to avoid), it was in response to the prayer of others. It obviously could not have had anything to do with any exercise of faith on my part — I was unconscious, both then and for many days after.

Comfort

Throughout the subsequent ordeal, it *really was* a wonderful comfort to know of the many people praying for me. And I somehow knew it before I was told of it. One of the first sensations I had when I "came to" in intensive care was the feeling, despite the misery, as if I were being uplifted by hundreds of hands. Somehow, below those hundreds of hands there seemed to be one large, all-encompassing pair of hands. And then there were the many beautiful, comforting Christian friends and visitors, not just family. There were even some people I had never known before, who came to express their love, and often their gratitude for the creation ministry I had been involved in.

Some non-Christian visitors came, too. One of my former patients somehow made her way, with her husband, through the phalanx of my family, formed to protect me from excessive visitor strain. It was quite a few weeks after the accident, and I shared with this couple how blessed I had been that the plastic (facial reconstructive) surgeon I had been assigned was regarded as the world's best. He was renowned for his charitable work in restoring the horribly deformed faces of some of the children in poorer countries in Australia's Asia-Pacific neighborhood. I recall a steady stream of visiting specialists at my bedside. Experts from places like Sweden, Britain, and the United States, they were eager to learn from some of his revolutionary new techniques.

The facial fractures I had suffered were grouped according to what is known as the "Le Fort" classification. One type was Le Fort 1, then there was Le Fort 2, and Le Fort 3. I had suffered all of them. Because of this, I would often be introduced as "the full hand." When I first saw a 3-D CAT scan of my skull, I quipped to someone that it looked like an ancient Aboriginal skull that had been exposed by the desert wind and had, for the past century or so, been kicked by every passing camel.[1]

Anyway, I was eagerly explaining to this former lady patient how fortunate I was that this leading specialist had performed his world-renowned operation on me, one which would greatly improve the results, and reduce the number, of operations needed subsequently. This procedure (performed

---

1 International readers may not be aware that Australia's feral camel population has long surpassed that of Arabia.

many weeks ago by that stage) had involved making an incision "from here to here" (I put my finger on top of one ear, and drew it up and around the top of my head to the top of the other ear). Then the face was dissected away from the bone, peeling it slowly downwards. The idea, I explained, was to expose the front of the skull, so that a team of several doctors, including an orthodontist, could get in there with their wires and screws and the like. The idea was that together, they would try to restore the "big picture" of the shattered bony architecture of the face; the details would be worked on in later procedures. The after-effects of this nine-hour, multi-man operation to "remove and repair" my face produced many days of the most intense, excruciating misery.

As I was describing what had been done, I guess I forgot that not all people can handle such "medical detail." I should have noticed this patient's husband leaning more and more heavily against the side of the room. By the time I looked up at him, I saw that he was a sickly grey-green color and was sliding down the wall into a crumpled heap on the floor.

I pressed the buzzer, holding it down longer than usual to alert the nursing staff. The head nurse rushed in, saying, "What's wrong, dear, what's your problem?" I remember pointing to the fainted body on the floor and saying, "It's not for me — *he* needs your help." I remember the strange look on her face, unsure whether she should laugh or not.

Chapter 5

What about Healing?

What, then, about the whole notion of divine healing, faith healing as it is so often called? Many would have us believe that to simply accept the Curse is not a New Testament view. If we ask in faith, they say, we have a *right* to expect healing. In that view, instead of spending six months in a hospital, I should have been able to expect to pick up my mattress and walk out of there, just like the paralyzed man in Mark 2:3–12. Because his paralysis was long-term, his useless limbs would have been dramatically wasted, their joints long since frozen by fibrous tissue growing across them.

I had massive muscle wasting after just a few weeks of inactivity. My 6-feet 3-inch (1.9 m) frame was down to 128 pounds (58 kg) at one stage. I recall being lowered into my first hospital bath and joking that I now knew how a *Stegosaurus* — the dinosaur with all those plates sticking up along his backbone — felt on bath nights. This was because I was exquisitely conscious of the bony vertebrae, exposed by the wasting of back muscle, poking against the back and bottom of the tub.

The dramatic healing in Mark's gospel thus involved more than just restoring damaged nerve connections. It also had to involve creating new muscle tissue and joint architecture. Some Christians balk at the notion of Christ creating the galaxies in a day. But stars and galaxies are actually rather simple in structure and information content compared to muscle cells — or, for that matter, dead fish, when Jesus fed the five thousand in Matthew 14. Over and over, John's gospel shows us how Jesus was identifying himself as the miracle-working Genesis Creator. He did not have to wait billions of years for natural processes to take place. "For he spoke, and it was done; he commanded, and it stood fast" (Ps. 33:9).

I hasten to say that this is not a treatise on this subject of healing. I mostly just want to share what happened to me, personally, which includes both healing (miraculous) and non-healing. I have found over and over that sharing this has been enlightening and encouraging to Christians struggling with this issue.

I am sometimes asked whether I "believe in healing." But this question is not carefully enough defined. Anyone who believes in the God that raised Jesus from the dead, and who healed so many of the sick and maimed instantly, *must*, to be consistent, believe that God is capable of healing supernaturally, even today, in response to prayer. There is also the exhortation to prayer for the healing of the sick in James 5:14. This passage will be more directly addressed in the next half of this book.

However, the questioner usually really means to ask whether one believes that Christians can expect what I call "demand healing" — that is, since Jesus' death was an overcoming of the Curse, all Christians, they say, have a right to expect total healing in response to prayer. Right now, they mean, not after His future coming in glory, with the removal of the Curse and the restoration of creation. However, all around us, we still see Christians sick and deteriorating. So this viewpoint of "if you have faith that you will be healed, you *will* be healed" has led to the framework of thought that, subtly if unintentionally, "blames the victim" for lack of faith, hardness of heart, and so on. I saw much tragedy and heartache in my Christian medical days from patients who had become convinced that their non-healing was a lack of faith, and were in total despair.

Healed Despite Lack of Faith

It was actually without much enthusiasm that I agreed to have healing prayer in the hospital. The huge hole over my right kneecap had never healed up, despite daily dressings. In fact, it had become infected with a multiply-resistant strain of *Klebsiella* bacteria. All antibiotics were useless.

This is common in major trauma care centers. When I was in intensive care, all of us in that unit had become colonized with a multi-resistant strain of "golden staph" as the layperson calls *Staphylococcus aureus*. Of the five of us patients involved, the four others were, one by one, carried out dead, doctors helpless to fight bacteria that laughed at their finest bug-killers. A sobering feeling, I can tell you. I was later able to use this experience, incidentally, to help show how these are not examples of evolution, but the opposite. So-called "supergerms" are in fact better called "superwimps."[1]

The surgeons had tried to heal the wound by covering it with a flap of live muscle. One of the two heads of my calf

---

1 *Creation* magazine 20(1):10-13, 1997, also <www.AnswersInGenesis.org/docs/337.asp>

muscle on that side, still attached to its original blood supply, was tunneled through to the front of the leg and then sewn on top of the gaping hole. But even this maneuver had failed. The entire knee was getting progressively redder and hotter, and it looked like I would have to have the whole leg amputated in a desperate attempt to stop the infection spreading into my bloodstream.

That night, with the decision due soon, I was visited by Irene, a family friend who was also a specialist in infections. In fact, she was the Deputy Director of Microbiology at the top government institution affiliated with the hospital I was in. The general practitioner-surgeon who had been my partner for years in family practice was her husband. Both had been towers of strength and comfort in this time of trial. Irene said, "Carl, I believe that the Lord has brought us to this point, where medicine has no more answers, to drive us to depend on Him alone." While she prayed, rebuking the germs in the name of the Lord Jesus, I was not exactly sparkling with faith. In fact, I recall thinking, *What would her boss think if he heard her now?* It was late at night — I did not even look at the knee afterward, and soon went into the usual fitful, drugged sleep. I had many more physical problems to distract my thoughts. The next morning, I was stunned to see all signs of infection in the knee gone. No redness, no swelling, no tenderness, nothing at all. Medically, it was incredible.

Later that morning, Irene came to see me on a ward round, accompanied by the director himself, her boss. He lifted off the sheet to examine my knee, and when he saw what had taken place, his brow furrowed: "What happened here?" Irene must have had talks with him before about the things of the Lord, because she just smiled sweetly and pointed skyward with her fingers. With an annoyed exclamation, he flung the covers back down again, turned, and hastened off.

I used to wonder how some of those who saw Jesus' healing miracles could still deny that He was who He claimed to be. But Jesus himself taught in Luke 16:31 that if someone is not inclined or willing to listen to God's Word (particularly "Moses and the prophets") then even someone being raised from the dead would not be enough to make them believe. I have seen more than once the truth of His words.

Not Healed Despite Lots of Faith

Not surprisingly, the experience with the knee made me much more enthusiastic when, later, a visiting hospital chaplain said she wanted to pray for my damaged eye, and was convinced that God wanted to heal it. At that stage, I could only see light and dark from that eye. The eye specialists had not shared with me fully the extent of the damage, saying only that there was a "blood clot" in the front of the eye, obstructing its view. We would have to "wait and see" how much sight I regained in it. My medical training made me fairly pessimistic about its future, though. So much so that I wrote to an insurance company predicting that I would probably lose it.

The insurance issue arose because I had found out that, despite all vehicles in Australia having compulsory insurance for third party bodily injury, I had no injury claim for this accident. Obviously, the accident was my "fault." But it also had to do with some complex situation concerning state regulations. My vehicle was registered in one state (South Australia), the other vehicle in another state (Victoria), while the accident had happened elsewhere again (the Northern Territory). So I had asked my family to bring in my insurance files, to see what private coverage I might have had in relation to my accident. I found a small policy which allowed $15,000 for the loss of one arm, one leg, or one eye, and $30,000 if *both* arms, legs, or eyes were lost. (As if losing both eyes were only twice as tragic as losing one!) The policy said I had only a limited time after whatever incident caused the loss of the eye to make the claim. It seemed to make no provision for a situation in which I might only lose the eye much later. So, in case I fell through another loophole here, I thought I would dictate a letter to my family to send to the company immediately. I told them about the situation and the impending loss of the eye, or at least that I might eventually discover that I would never regain the sight in it. This is all relevant, as we will see shortly, to another way in which I saw God's providential involvement in my situation.

As soon as the letter was mailed, I was putting the policy back into my bedside drawer when I noticed something scribbled on it in my handwriting in faint pencil: "Cancelled 1976." *Oh, well,* I thought, *so much for that wasted effort.* Just in case, I asked a family member to call my insurance broker, who confirmed that I had indeed cancelled that policy ten years earlier. But more on that later.

Here I was, then, having my eye prayed for, only this time I was also praying right alongside, earnestly and passionately believing that it would be healed. Had I not seen wonders at least as great on my own body? But nothing changed. And a few days later, I received some additional bad news. There is a well-known but mysterious phenomenon, called "sympathetic ophthalmia" (eye inflammation), that sometimes happens when an eye suffers a penetrating injury.[2] For some reason, the eye that was *not* injured can

---

2 Sometimes also known as sympathetic ophthalmitis, it may be caused by an auto-immune reaction to uveal pigment.

become inflamed, as if in "sympathy" with the damaged one. The only known cure is to remove the injured eye, even if it can still see well. If this is not done as a semi-emergency procedure, *both* eyes will quickly become blind. Louis Braille, the inventor of the Braille system that allows reading by the blind, was afflicted in this way as a child.

Missionary surgeons working in Papua New Guinea have told me of the difficulty they face in this sort of situation. It is not uncommon in the New Guinean "bush" for a child to run into a sharp twig that penetrates the eye. The injury may appear minor and seem to heal. Imagine the parents' doubts and disbelief when told that their child has to have this apparently healthy, visually functioning eye removed, or else go blind.

The doctor who was checking my eyes every day had just noticed the first signs of this mysterious inflammation in my good eye. Suddenly, I was faced with the choice that was not a choice; to have my damaged eye taken out ("How soon, doc?" "Yesterday!") or go blind.

I have known of instances in Western countries where Christians were urged that if they agreed to have their damaged eye removed, this would be a serious lack of faith — they needed to "keep on believing" that it would be healed. Fortunately, most heeded their doctors' strident warnings. Tragically, where they listened to their well-intentioned friends instead, blindness has resulted. Imagine the dual possibilities of ongoing mental torment for those unfortunate individuals; regret about one's decision, and the doubt about what might be wrong with one's faith.

So, instead of the eye being healed after that fervent prayer, I had now lost it. This highlights why many find my experiences in regard to healing encouraging whenever I share them. They can see the sovereignty of God in healing.

He healed, supernaturally and totally, parts of me — yet other parts He did not heal. That seems to square with the "whole counsel of God," putting together the various passages in the Bible that relate to healing. It also squares with the fact that in all churches, including those which teach "demand-healing," one glance at the congregation confirms that, like all the rest of us, they are still under the Curse. Their skin elasticity continues to degenerate, their arteries slowly clog up (hastened often by bad eating habits), their joints deteriorate and, if one could "see" inside them, or indeed any group of people, many would undoubtedly have evidence of diseases such as diabetes and early, as-yet-undetected malignancies.

Is Healing Our Right?

I have no "right" to demand anything from God, apart from what He has clearly and unambiguously promised to me. All of what I may lay claim to is totally undeserved, all earned by God in Christ on my behalf. It includes the complete forgiveness of my sin, and the immense and eternal riches of being a joint heir with Christ. It includes the joy unspeakable of knowing that, with the rest of the invisible church, the body of Christ, I will be in wonderful, sinless fellowship and co-regency with Him throughout all the ages to come, without end. Why then does God ask us to pray for healing? Why does He ask us to pray for anything at all, if it is all a matter of His sovereign will as to which of these petitions He will grant and which He will not? It is presumptuous, if not dangerous, to speculate about the ways of God, beyond that which He chooses to reveal to us. But we do see in the Bible a pattern in which God wants people to pray, even chooses them to petition Him, so that He might choose one course of action rather than the other. I think this has something to do with praying "in His name," i.e., according to His will.

On one occasion in the Old Testament, God said that He looked for someone to stand before Him in the gap, on behalf of the land, so that He might not destroy it (Ezek. 22:30). It was His will that someone should pray in a particular way, in other words. To us, limited to only those representations of the infinite God which our finite minds can grasp, it seems very strange that God should seek for someone to persuade Him to change His mind. But the Psalmist gives a further insight when he says, "Therefore he said that he would destroy them, had not Moses his chosen stood before him in the breach, to turn away his wrath, lest he should destroy them" (Ps. 106:23).

Neither wisdom, qualification, courage, nor the space available, permit me to venture more fully into the mysterious connection between God's sovereign will and man's choices. But notice that even where Moses "changed God's mind," the intercessor was nevertheless the one chosen by God in the first place. When Christ intercedes for us as our advocate before the Father, He does so as one chosen by the Father for precisely that purpose.

Even when I pray for something and it comes to pass, I like to think that I am careful to avoid "taking credit" for having prayed. I think it is more in tune with the thrust of what the Bible teaches about God to regard even my prayer as having somehow fulfilled God's will, as having been sought and in a sense made to pass by Him.

Again, do such fine distinctions and contemplations matter? Or are they just academic? I recall that the peace they gave me, when about to be wheeled into the operating room to remove my eye, and immediately after the procedure, was a powerful influence on those looking on. I have never had so many unbelievers coming to me to ask about the things of God. In the midst of this great personal weakness, I have never felt more empowered in the vital spiritual area of sharing about Christ.

I recall one nurse, obviously not a Christian, commending me for how my faith sustained me. She said, "My mother is also a woman of great faith, but I can't go her way." I asked her what she meant. She said that her mother, a devout Roman Catholic, had been abandoned by her husband, the nurse's father. "Ever since then, she's lived in complete faith that he will come back to her. There's no sign of it, and he lives with someone else now, but she still hangs on. She says she really believes that God will bring him back, if she believes it enough, and she does, so He will. I guess I admire her for her faith, but I couldn't do it."

I sensed that she saw her mother's "faith" as somehow representative of what being a Christian was all about — admirable in a way, but also somehow unreal and off the planet. I tried to sensitively point out that the only thing we can claim authoritatively about Christian faith is what God has chosen to reveal to us in His Word, the Bible. By that standard, her mother's "faith" seemed to be really just a blind choice to believe in something in pursuit of personal wish-fulfillment. The Bible makes it clear that faith is not blind. The heroes of faith listed in Hebrews 11 did not wake up one morning and decide "I want to believe something, so I will. I want to believe that I will be wealthy, healthy, or happy, and if I have enough faith, it will happen." Nor did God grant such wishes so that they would then live happily ever after.

Noah would have rightly been regarded as a madman if he had chosen to believe that God would destroy the world with a global flood, just because that suited Noah's circumstances. Abraham's desire for a son and heir was more than reasonable and understandable. But what if he had simply awakened one morning and said, "Well, my aged wife is obviously not capable of bearing children, but I'm going to *believe* that God will give me a son, and so He will." Would he have been a man of great faith, in the biblical sense, or just a nut case? Both Noah and Abraham could only be commended for their faith because they were relying on a promise that God had clearly and unmistakably made to them. Abraham had been told by God, specifically and directly, that his wife would bear a son, despite her age. It was not based on a fantasy-wish, as in this nurse's mother's case. God had not promised that He would return her husband to her.

The understanding I have shared in these few pages has been an attempt to shed some light on the interaction between faith and prayer (and their results or lack of them) with the will of God. I have found repeatedly that it has made a powerful difference in the lives of people, especially suffering Christians who wonder why God does not grant their desires.

Chapter 6

Amazing Provision

I promised earlier that the story of the letter to the insurance company would become relevant. If I had known that the policy was cancelled, I would never have sent that letter, obviously. Shortly after my eye had indeed been lost, I recall telling a Christian GP (general practitioner) friend how ironic it was that I had planned to build a pool at our new home in tropical Cairns. Daily exercising in water would have been ideal rehabilitation for my stiff, wasted right leg in the months after I would eventually go home. But now, with my forcibly revised income circumstances, the $14,500 quoted for this pool was out of reach. My friend, a very godly older man, sensed that I was not bitter. But I was wondering, nevertheless, whether it was right to pray for a pool. It seemed to me a bit like praying for a BMW or similar luxury item. He assured me that, under the circumstances, it was a most appropriate thing to pray for. And so we did.

A few days later, I received a letter from the insurance company. I read the expected words: "Our records indicate that you have not paid the premium amount of $77 on this policy for the last ten years." Okay, let's get it over with — no premium, no policy, no claim, right? Then came the astonishing part. "If you send us a check for $770 representing ten years' premiums, we will process your claim." No, this was ridiculous! It couldn't mean what it seemed to mean. No insurance company could survive like this, no matter how well-intentioned. "Your house has just burnt down, and you haven't insured with us for years? Never mind, just send us all the premiums you would have paid us had you thought of insuring with us, and we'll cough it up anyway." Sure. This must be a ploy to get the $770, and then I would be told that after checking my claim, obviously they couldn't pay, blah blah. . . . But — why would they word it this way?

Cautiously, I dictated another letter in which I said that I had indeed lost the eye and the written medical evidence was enclosed. Here was my check for the $770, but it was given on the understanding that their letter meant that they would pay the claim and if it meant otherwise, please return the sorely needed $770, etc. Anyway, without any further comment from the insurance company, back came their check for $15,000! We committed to building that pool after all. Whenever I swam in that pool, I would remember the marvelous way in which God provided it, in answer to that prayer. As it was being built, when the excavating machine had finished digging out the ground for the pool, I joked to the family that this hole in the ground represented the hole in my head where my eye used to be (they were familiar with my macabre sense of humor).

Actually, losing my eye was a tougher experience than I thought it would be. Not so much losing the sight in it; I had not had any real sight in it to speak of for months. It was the idea that this little moist globe, part of that which seemed to define "me" in a way which the poets express as a "window to one's soul," would be gone forever. A part of my body since I was born, it would not be with me anymore. Instead, there would be this gaping, unnatural hole. I was still trying not to think of it on the night after the operation when the comment by the night nurse brought it rudely home again. Finding me awake long after "lights out," she said, unthinkingly but accurately, "Now, dear, you really must close your *eye* and go to sleep." The tiny replacement, in this common idiom, of the plural by the singular stung savagely. I knew she meant no harm by it, though.

The next day, a Christian friend came to see me. He had just heard that after all the other trials of the preceding months, I had now lost the eye as well. He said, obviously deeply empathetic, "Oh, Carl, you really needed this latest thing like a hole in the head." Immediately, he struck his forehead with his palm, mortified. "Oh, no, what have I just said? I didn't mean it . . . ." I thought it was one of those brilliant inadvertent comedy lines, and laughingly reassured him that I was getting over it. I had been "toughened" by the rude reminder of the night before. When I told him about the nurse's comment, he found it rather funny, which I did by then, too.

Death in General

What if I had really died in the accident or shortly afterwards? Many would have said that it was "unfair" for God to take the life of one so young. A few years back, a collapsing slagheap tragically suffocated many school children in a Welsh mining town. There was a worldwide outpouring of not just grief, but a railing against God's "unfairness" because of their young ages. Or when floods wipe out thousands of people, including children, in some village somewhere, the same questions are raised. But think on this. Is it any "fairer" for an old person to die than a young one? It is somehow seen as more reasonable, or more natural, he or she has had more of a "fair go" at life. But is death at any age "natural"? Or is it just that we are so used to living in a sin-cursed, decaying world that we resign ourselves to it in old age?

Let's be honest. If you were a sprightly 70, and found out that you were condemned to die tomorrow, would you shrug your shoulders and just casually accept it on account of your age? If you could have some special advanced genetic engineering done, and keep living a healthy life for many hundreds of years, would you not eagerly seize the opportunity? I suggest that, deep down at least, we all realize that death at any age is an abomination, not the way things were meant to be or should be.

We tend to readily ask why God allows thousands to die at once when there is an earthquake in Turkey, a terrorist act in the United States, or floods in Bangladesh. But in the time you have taken to read this book to this point, many, many thousands of people have died across the whole world. If it is "unfair" for God to allow death in the case of these "concentrated" occurrences of death in one spot, why is it any more fair when the thousands of deaths are spread out across the globe? I suggest that it does not really change the real philosophical question of "why does God allow death?" for which, as we have seen, the answer's in Genesis.

To put it another way, let's say that you have concluded that it would have been "fair" for God to prevent the deaths of the school children in Wales. Then, to be really "fair," He should prevent all deaths of school-age children in accidents, anywhere. Having done that, we would then conclude that it was "unfair" for Him to allow childhood deaths from disease. So let's assume that He chose to prevent all deaths in children, anywhere, anytime. But if He chose to define childhood as ending at 18, why would it now be "fair" to allow a 19 year old to die? I hope this abstract "thought experiment" makes it clear that we could not be satisfied, logically, until death had been eliminated altogether.

Which brings us right back to the point that death is an intruder, an outrage. When Jesus contemplated His recently dead friend, Lazarus, He wept. The Greek word used implies tears of rage, not compassion. Even though He knew that He would shortly resurrect Lazarus, the real issue was that death should not be present at all, and would not have been, if not for human rebellion. The reality was that Lazarus would only be given a temporary reprieve from death, anyway. Bottom line — the only way that God can be truly "fair" is to do exactly what He will do — create another perfect world in which there can be no more death and suffering of any kind, at all.

But it is not possible for us to enter that perfect new creation carrying our sin natures, or we would soon ruin it, too. He had to make a way to take our sin away forever, through the perfect sacrifice of the Lord Jesus Christ, God the Son, God's sinless Lamb bearing the penalty of God's wrath on our behalf.

"There's Always Someone Worse Off"

From my several non-Christian visitors, I experienced firsthand the "world's" attempts to give comfort in suffering. All of them well-meaning, they would usually say something like, "Well, there's always someone worse off." I tried to imagine what this hypothetical "someone" was going through, and why that should somehow make me feel better. In fact, it made things worse, and not only because I felt sorry for this person. I thought to myself that this "someone" was being told the same thing, that there was someone worse off — and that would certainly be true. But that "worse off" person would then have someone worse off still, and so on. Inevitably, one would have to come to the bottom of the pile, to an immensely pitiable individual undergoing who knows what unimaginable torment. (Maybe I had too much time on my hands — hospitals have a way of doing that to you after a while.)

This secular attempt at succor for the suffering was understandable, and in a way it mimicked the biblical notion of thankfulness (in the sense here of being thankful for not being worse off than one was). But the thankfulness I referred to earlier as mandatory for the Christian is subtly, but profoundly, different. Ephesians 5:20 tells us we are to give thanks "for (about, concerning) all things." I have heard this verse expounded to mean that in order to secure God's favor, we need to actually thank Him for calamity that befalls us. You know, to act and speak as if we are grateful that our child has died, or our body is being eaten up by malignancy. As if there is some magic formula in perversity, in seeming to go against everything reasonable and sensible, let alone the feelings raging inside of us. I am convinced (and it is equally consistent with the Greek construction) that we Christian believers are, instead, to give thanks *concerning* all circumstances that may befall us — which includes being thankful for the many things that are still ours, regardless (e.g., Eph. 1:3–7). Part of this being thankful *about* all circumstances is the knowledge that, in spite of any tragedy that may strike, God is still working His purposes for good (Rom. 8:28). To support all this, note that 1 Thessalonians 5:18 uses the same Greek root words *eucharisteo* (give thanks) and *pas* (everything). But it specifically has the preposition *en*, which ensures the meaning "in." That is, the meaning here is specifically narrowed to saying "*in* everything give thanks."

I don't mean just being thankful in a general, attitudinal sense, but literally, actively, positively thanking God. Once we get away from the notion that God owes us anything, we will start to lose our focus on what we have lost, and focus instead on being grateful for all the many blessings of daily life. So I couldn't walk properly anymore? Praise Him that I could breathe freely again, despite the damage to my chest and lungs. My face was smashed up? What a wonderful thing to be able to thank Him that my spinal cord was uninjured. How easy it would have been, in such a serious smash, to have ended up in a wheelchair, like famous Christian quadriplegic author Joni Eareckson-Tada, unable to brush a fly from the end of my nose. Thanks so much Lord, that I can do that — right now — see, I can touch it now and revel in my thankfulness to You, Father.

In the years following the accident, there has been just so much to be thankful for. Not just Lisa's amazing preservation and my own unlikely survival, but even things that seem so minor, but mean so much. People are often surprised to hear me say that, if I ever start to feel sorry for myself in regard to my (really fairly minor) infirmities now, it makes a big difference when I remember to thank Him once again for — wait for it — being able to turn on my side to go to sleep! Sound trivial? It wouldn't if you had experienced what it was like to be in a traction apparatus for months, unable to lie in any position other than flat on your back. I find that those who have experienced this know *exactly* what I mean.

Chapter 7

Who's in Charge, Anyway?

The thankfulness discussed in the last chapter extends also to my having had the opportunity to see some of the outworkings of the way in which my particular misfortune was used by God for good. In February 1987, ten months after the accident, the Queensland-based creation ministry (then called *Creation Science Foundation* or CSF), of which I had long been a de facto "southern wing," suffered a major blow. There were sustained attempts to undermine the ministry in the face of its supporters, in association with the resignation of a prominent leadership figure.

The other major figure in CSF's leadership, Ken Ham (co-author of this book) had only recently taken up residence in the United States at the request of the CSF Board. Time has shown how vital that step was, as it has blossomed into a worldwide outreach, now based in the Cincinnati region. Following the above-mentioned crisis, CSF, suddenly leaderless, was tottering badly, its supporters confused and disillusioned. Financial support had slowed to a trickle. Humanly speaking, Ken would have to come back to Australia to restore confidence in the leadership. That would be the end of his establishment of a beachhead in the influential (for better or for worse) realm of American Christendom.

Soon after all this happened, Ken flew to my bedside. He urged me to consider coming into the ministry to take over the leadership in Australia. My name was already known through the magazine and so on, so I was a natural choice. It would just be "for a while," he said, until the ministry had stabilized.

Humanly speaking, if the revolt in CSF had happened at any other time in my life, I would have found it incredibly difficult, if not impossible, to leave what I saw as my main calling, being a Christian family doctor, which I loved deeply. If the request had come a few years later, I would have been back into my practice, this time in Cairns. But I knew that it was pointless to open a practice until the worst of the series of operations I was facing had finished. It was not fair or realistic to expect people to commit their allegiance to a doctor who was planning to shut the doors every few weeks for another round of surgery on himself. So after some prayer and a deep breath, I said I would do it.

I knew that it would involve traveling to town after town, sometimes for weeks on end, even while on crutches, and the ministry could not afford to send anyone with me. But I also knew how vital the work was. It was clear that God had put me in a position where it was pointless to ask what His will was. His will was laid out in the Bible, namely that we should do what we can to win souls for Christ. Given such a need, and faced with such a request, and the unique "pause" in my life, what else was there to do? The rest is history, including the fact that the ministry and its growth have kept me so busy that there was no time to ever return to medicine.

The Bible and Decision-making

While on the subject of "God's will," my mother told me that when I was unconscious in intensive care, she was watching her mangled son lie there on a respirator with a tube in his neck, a Christian acquaintance of mine at her side. She heard him say, "You can just see God screaming at him that it was against God's will for him to have gone to Queensland." Leaving the insensitivity of the comment's timing to one side, it highlights a common issue among believers. That is the belief that there is a "perfect will of God" for our lives. Not referring here to the obvious moral issues, which it is God's will that we obey, but to such things as which school we will attend, which job we will undertake, and so on.

Now of course God is obviously the "boss" of everything that happens. But the usual way in which this "God's will" matter is seen is that it is something which we are able to either implement or frustrate. In other words, it is (even if only implicitly) as if the burden is on us to discern this mysterious, specific, one and only route at every step along the way. Worse, there is a corollary, spoken or unspoken, in that if we do not correctly discern this perfect will, we will, at the least, miss out on "God's best." At worst, we will get "zapped" in retribution, as had now happened to me so far as this man was concerned.

Of course, I'm not denying that there are circumstances in which God specifically directs or graciously confirms some particular direction. But this seems to go much beyond that. It is not clearly spelled out in Scripture exactly how we are supposed to discern this alleged "perfect will."

The advice given in much Christian literature is thus of necessity vague, sometimes under the heading of "three harbor lights in a row." The words of the Bible are invoked as one of these lights, but never as clear teaching, and often used semi-superstitiously (i.e., "I was contemplating which of three Bible colleges to go to, and I noticed that my devotional that very morning was about a verse which had in it the word 'harvest.' That's also a part of the name of one of these colleges. Isn't it exciting?") Another one is the advice of others, and the third "harbor light" is usually one's own inner "peace."

The problem is that there is so much subjectivity in all this, and no objective biblical platform on which to anchor things. Our fallible, fallen feelings are notoriously unreliable. We are not exhorted by God to trust our emotions, but to trust only His Word, the Bible.

Associated with all this is the temptation to judge the rightness or wrongness of a decision not on biblical grounds but on what happens afterward, on how one is "blessed" or otherwise. But this denies the biblical teaching that the wicked may indeed prosper, as mentioned earlier, and that the rain falls on the just *and* the unjust (Matt. 5:45).

I have known of "splits" in churches and ministries from various causes in which many people have refused to judge the issue causing the split on biblical criteria. Instead, they wait to see which of the two "offspring" of the formerly unified body ends up being more "blessed" by God in terms of growing and prospering. But this seems to be a completely wrongheaded approach. Some of the worst cults (theologically speaking) are large and wealthy, so by this criterion of "blessing" they must be more right than others that have not done so well.

As I read my Bible, there are moral and immoral choices, but these are judged as such by the clear guidelines given in the Word. When it comes to which city to live in, or which Bible college to go to, or what job to choose, there are only wise and foolish choices, not sin or non-sin. God *promises* wisdom (not the same as intelligence) to those who ask (James 1:5). And even if one makes a foolish choice, a Christian is still a child of God, heir to all the promises of God. Great calamity or great blessing may befall one in this life, neither of which may have had anything to do with one's recent decisions.

Space does not permit a full exposition on this aspect, so I won't be surprised if the reader doesn't agree on all points.[1] Suffice it to say that, before working these issues through biblically, I had in fact held to the traditional "harbor lights" view. I agonized in prayer for many months over the decision to move.

Whatever one's position on this, it seems clear that God used the accident to bring me into the ministry. I have said that I wished He had sent me a letter, or writing on the wall. I believe I would have listened. But it is His sovereign right, if He so chooses, to use a collision with a truck to do so instead. That is why I said that I am thankful to have been able to see the good while in this life.

Romans 8:28 makes it clear that *all* things work together for good to believers. That must, then, apply to the bad things that happen as well as the good. The problem is that we naturally want to be able to *see* the good things, to

---

1 A brief, helpful essay on the topic may be found at <<www.ariel.org/ff00142c.html>>

find out "why" before we get to heaven. In the case of the tragic illness which struck down Ken Ham's brother Robert, dealt with in the following chapters, it would have been particularly hard to try to see the good. A 42-year-old family man, with the promise of being one of the great preachers of our age, cut off in his prime by a cruel disease that wastes his brain and robs him of speech and eventually all human dignity and personality. But note that Romans 8:28 only says that things will work together for good. It does not specify that this will necessarily be for our good in this life, nor does it specify that the fulfillment of this promise will become obvious to us this side of eternity. Abraham, that great man of faith, was promised a huge swath of land for him and his descendants. Yet in his lifetime, the only land he owned was a small plot just large enough to bury his wife. The Promised Land only became available to his descendants centuries later.

Cockroaches, Princess Diana, and God's Sovereignty

On this whole topic of things working together for good, I remember being asked to preach a Good Friday sermon at Robert Ham's church in his temporary absence. It was not long after an accident in a French tunnel had ended the life of the Princess of Wales. I thought to myself, *Well, I obviously need to somehow make it relevant to the whole issue of Easter, the Cross, and the Resurrection, but they will be going in there only half-awake, expecting to hear the traditional message about a story they're all familiar with.* I walked up to the pulpit and looked around. The audience demeanor confirmed that most were not exactly enthusiastically expectant. Some looked only half-awake. Let's face it, going to church on Good Friday is often a tradition, an expectation. But when I announced the title, which was "The Cockroach

That Killed Princess Diana," every eye suddenly shot wide open. I had their attention that morning.

It went something like this (greatly condensed):

> You've all heard of the butterfly effect, where a butterfly flaps its wings in Argentina, and it "causes" a tornado to hit northern Kentucky months later. It's part of what's known as chaos theory, in which tiny things can have major effects that could not be predicted from the initial conditions. Not that the butterfly's wings actually generate the energy for the tornado, that energy is all in the atmosphere.
>
> The point is that because the butterfly flaps its wings, one tiny puff of air goes in one direction instead of another, which might interact with another atmospheric thing, and so on until you have an effect that is out of all proportion to its apparent cause. If the butterfly had not flapped its wings, a different set of events entirely would have happened in the atmosphere. So the whole complex pattern of happenings in the atmosphere is the result of an incredible number of small events interacting and adding up in ways that are too mindbogglingly complex for humans to understand. In the same way, human interactions and the things that play out in our lives can also have the most major things coming from tiny "butterfly effects."
>
> What if a dead cockroach fell off a bench in China, startled a butterfly, which flapped its wings, so that months later, a storm struck a part of Europe instead of hitting farther south? That

meant (in this fictitious scenario) that Diana's cook had to cancel his planned holiday at that time, and take it at another time, which meant that her favorite dessert wasn't available to her, which meant she left the meal a few minutes earlier. If it had been later, the car which clipped her would not have been coming at that time.... It is not hard to construct any number of "what ifs" such that in one sense, a cockroach could indeed have been "responsible" for killing the princess.

If the coffee I had with lunch the day of my accident had been a few degrees hotter, it would have taken me longer to drink. Humanly speaking, that would have meant "no accident." A few seconds before or after the precise time when the truck was coming the other way, and my falling asleep would have probably been a harmless, if embarrassing, event. There was no other traffic to speak of. The bumping of my vehicle as it ran across the desert sands would have quickly alerted its occupants to what was happening.

The point is that there is a near-infinite cascade of "butterfly events" leading up to anything that happens, and only the infinite, omniscient God knows of, and is able to orchestrate, every one of those complex interactions. Who knows what myriad minor things in their background resulted in the Roman soldiers having the impulse to gamble over the clothing of the crucified Christ? Yet in so doing, they were fulfilling the precise prophecy given many centuries before.

What does this have to do with Romans 8:28, in which we're told that all things work together for good to those who love God? Simply that there are countless ways in which even a bad thing might be used of God to work for some other good, even in some far away continent, ways that we might never see or hear of. We, or our descendants, *might* be able to see the good in this life, as in the example in Ken Ham's section. But we should not fret when we cannot, because we can still be totally secure in God's comforting promise that somehow, some way, He will bring good out of it in the "big picture," the eternal mosaic that only He can truly oversee.

In reality, the Bible has never promised us a rose garden, as the song goes. When we grasp the Genesis "big picture," of a fallen world groaning in hope for its redemption, we can understand at last. We are truly living in the land of the dying. God's Word does not tell us that we will *never* "walk through the valley of the shadow of death," as the beloved "Shepherd's Psalm" (23) puts it. But it does tell us that when we do walk through that valley, and indeed any of life's valleys, He will be with us, to comfort us and deliver us from all need to fear (v. 4).

Because of what happened at the Cross, those who believe can know that this world, with all its apparent injustice, pain, and suffering, will be replaced by a new creation, with new heavens and a new earth where all these things will be no more. The Bible asks, rhetorically through Abraham in Genesis 18:25, "Shall not the judge of all the earth do right?" In the eternal "big picture," we can be sure that the books *will* all balance. From God's perspective, which is the only one that counts, no injustice or unfairness will have prevailed in the slightest.

This is why you, as a Christian, can truly say, as David does in the sixth verse of that same Psalm 23, "Surely goodness and mercy [love, kindness] shall follow me all the days of my life." Not that we can be sure that no sickness or disaster will befall us, or that we will be immune from financial loss, but because the goodness and mercy that really counts, and that is in focus here, is the goodness and mercy of the Lord to us in bestowing His everlasting, undeserved love on the believer — for eternity. Consistent with this, the verse goes on to end with "And I will dwell in the house of the LORD for ever."

Preaching which promises the unbeliever that coming to Christ will buy him or her some sort of insurance from all troubles here on earth is tragically misleading, even if well-meant. So, too, is the preaching to believers that makes them think that their lot in life is to have health, wealth, and happiness. I think a fitting way of closing here may be to contemplate the words of the apostle Paul, addressing believers in Romans 8:35–39.

Paul asks:

> Who shall separate us from the love of Christ? Shall trouble or hardship or persecution or famine or nakedness or danger or sword? As it is written: "For your sake we face death all day long; we are considered as sheep to be slaughtered." No, in all these things we are more than conquerors through him who loved us.

Notice that the Bible does *not* say that we will have an absence of hardship and suffering, but rather that *in* all these things we have the victory. Why? Because no matter what befalls — and it is the ultimate comforting reality, as millions of Christians have found — our eternal heritage is secure. Paul goes on to say:

> For I am convinced that neither death nor life, neither angels nor demons, neither the present

nor the future, nor any powers, neither height nor depth, nor anything else in all creation, will be able to separate us from the love of God that is in Christ Jesus our Lord.

Amen.

Part Two

Sickness, Suffering, and Death —— "Normal" in an Abnormal World

Ken Ham

Chapter 1

A Cruel Fate

On the telephone 10,000 miles away, my sister described my brother's physical appearance this way: "Do you remember those TV programs that showed those horrible pictures of prisoners from the concentration camps? Remember how thin they looked from starvation? Well, in a way, Robert reminds me of them." This was the result of a degenerative brain disease, a type of dementia.

I wanted to see my younger brother at least one more time. He was so young — early forties — how could this be happening to him? I boarded a plane for 20 hours of flying — lots of time to reflect on the past and contemplate the future.

A few hours after arriving in Australia, my heart began to race as I walked into the nursing home with my mother after my surprise visit. I hadn't seen Robert for a few months and I knew that no matter how hard I tried, I would not be prepared for what I was about to experience.

It was a pathetic sight. I gazed around a room of a dozen or so mostly elderly people. One lady whistled continually, while another kept saying certain words over and over again. Periodic groans were heard from another, and beside her another lady kept moving her legs and body in a peculiar continual motion. Some sat motionless, their contorted faces and glassy eyes glued on the television. Only one person seemed aware of my presence and spoke something unintelligible.

Inside, my heart was breaking. I thought about the fact that I was looking at someone's wife and mother, a husband and father, a son or daughter. As I entered some of the rooms, on the walls I saw pictures of some of these people before the horrible sicknesses overtook them. The contrast was so stark it was hard to believe I was looking at the same people.

This was a Christian nursing home. Most of these patients were dedicated Christians — maybe Sunday school teachers or deacons. One 78-year-old man in a room nearby had been an active evangelist. His family was gathered around him as he was breathing his last after a seven-year battle with Alzheimer's disease.

Then I saw Robert. He was lying there, hardly moving. He showed very little (if any) signs of any recognition of his mother and eldest brother. Mum tenderly stroked his forehead and then began the arduous task of trying to get him to swallow a special drink she had prepared for him. Increasingly, his swallowing ability was disappearing. His food had to be put through a blender and fed to him teaspoon by teaspoon, or through a drinking cup.

He would swallow and then choke. Mum would wipe his face and wait for the next opportunity to get him to take another sip. At times, tears would run down my mother's face. She was so patient and so loving, talking to him and caring for him just as one would for a baby. At times, we both held his hands. He would look at us and once or twice. I wondered whether I saw a flash of recognition in his facial expressions — and then it was gone.

My mind went back to our childhood. I vividly remember the good times when we played together, and special times when our parents took us camping and the fun of erecting a tent. One doesn't usually think about death at that time of one's life. Even growing up as a teenager, I had to attend a funeral or two, but it still doesn't really hit you that this could happen to you or someone very close to you. But the older I get, the more I have to deal with the death of people I have known intimately. The issue of death and separation from a loved one or special friend really begins to hit home. The first time I had to face such a thing was when my father died. Now I was facing the death of my brother, someone younger in age than myself.

Why would a loving and all-powerful God allow a dedicated man of God to be struck down in the prime of life, with a dreadful, dehumanizing disease that caused him to lose his mental faculties and muscular function, and die slowly as his family watched, helpless to do anything but agonize daily?

"But he was such a great preacher; he stood firmly on the Word of God; he preached the gospel; he wouldn't knowingly compromise God's Word," said my mother. "I still don't understand why God would allow this to happen to him!" she continued.

These thoughts and my mother's words continued to echo through my mind, as they had done as I stepped on to the plane to fly from the USA to Australia to see my brother for perhaps the last time on this earth.

Chapter 2

Confronting the Tragedy

I loved my brother Robert. We had much in common — both of us were in Christian work, teaching the Word of God. I had many conversations with Rob over the years on the telephone as we discussed theological issues. However, there came a time when my wife noticed that as I got off the telephone, I became increasingly frustrated about my conversations with him. "I don't understand," I would often say, "he is becoming so difficult to deal with."

As time went on, various family members told me that Rob was suffering from great stress resulting from his position as a pastor. Many were noticing changes in his behavior. One day I received a very disturbing phone call from one of my best friends. He attended Rob's church, even though he lived over an hour away, because he loved Rob's verse-by-verse Bible teaching. On this particular day, he took some of his visiting relatives to that church, but was greatly disturbed because the sermon Rob gave seemed to lack logic and was very disjointed. He told me that the sermon basically didn't make sense.

Not long after this, when I called Rob on the phone, he would tell me people were leaving the church. Time after time I was told another family had left. I couldn't understand what was happening. Those around him kept saying he was suffering from severe stress. Eventually, friends and family convinced Rob to go on leave to rest and recuperate. We all realized something serious was wrong, but none of us were prepared for what was subsequently found out after a barrage of tests over many months. He would never again preach the Word of God as he had so loved to do.

At age 43, Rob was diagnosed with a degenerative brain disease for which there was no earthly cure.

I remember the day I received the phone call from his wife, Brenda. We had hoped his brain tests would come back negative, and were all fairly sure that his problems were because of severe stress. However, the tests came back positive. Rob had a major problem — an unusual disease causing relentlessly progressive loss of brain function.

I didn't know what to say. My mind was in a daze. This couldn't be happening — not to Rob. Surely God wouldn't let this happen to a man who had sacrificed much to study and preach His Word? He had basically only just started his ministry — he was in the prime of life. At a time when there are so many Christian leaders who compromise the Word of God, and thus undermine its authority, my brother was totally committed to standing for its full authority. Why would God allow this to happen to *him* of all people? Where is the just, all-powerful God of the Bible in all of this?

I must admit that from a human perspective, none of this seemed to make sense. One of those heart-gripping emotional moments that I'll never forget, that has been indelibly impressed on my mind, was the time I took Robert to a local shopping center. By this time the disease had taken quite a hold and he couldn't speak much. He was difficult to control and wanted to wander off and grab things out of the stores. Just dealing with this, and watching a man who had been so upright in character do things we had to apologize for, was heart-wrenching. I only experienced an infinitesimally small amount of this compared to what his wife and children had to put up with. What were they feeling, having to deal with this day after day concerning their husband and father? Only those who have lived through such a horrific ordeal could even begin to understand what they must have gone through.

How could anyone reconcile these events with what Rob preached concerning a God who cares for us and loves us with an infinite love?

At the shopping center, Rob sat down with me to eat one of his favorite meals — Aussie meat pie and "mushy" peas. Suddenly, Rob saw some people in Muslim garb walking by. He jumped up and ran to them. "Wrong, wrong!" he shouted out. I gripped the table and held back the tears. Rob stared at the Muslims. They stopped and looked perplexed. "Wrong, wrong," he continued to say. Even though Rob couldn't communicate properly, he still had that burden to tell Muslims the truth about God — he wanted to see them saved — but he couldn't say any more than that. I ran to Rob and led him away from them, my heart breaking. "Lord," I said quietly, "I don't understand. He wants to tell them about You — why can't he do that? Why have You let this happen to him? It just doesn't make sense to me."

As I despairingly looked at Rob, my mind went back to the time when he was a bank manager. He was very successful and climbed up the ladder rather quickly. He had a great future in this financial institution. He had a secure job with an excellent salary and many other benefits. However, Rob would often tell me his real burden was to preach. Just like our father, he loved the Word of God and it greatly distressed him to see preachers who did not believe it and teach it like they should. Rob was deeply involved in his local church — he began lay preaching. He read and reread sermons by some of the greats like Martyn Lloyd-Jones[1] and Charles Haddon Spurgeon.[2]

During that time, my wife and I went full-time into the creation ministry now known as *Answers in Genesis*. Rob and his wife, Brenda, often gave us much-needed financial support. In those days the ministry was very small and finances were rather scarce. Rob and Brenda's financial support helped us more than they realized.

As the burden on Rob to preach increased, he believed God had very definitely called him to leave the bank and go to a theological college so he could study God's Word and become a teacher of the Bible.

1　D. Martyn Lloyd-Jones (1898–1981). A physician turned preacher, he became a colleague and successor to G. Campbell Morgan at Westminster Chapel in London in 1938. Upon Morgan's retirement in 1943, Lloyd-Jones became pastor of Westminster Chapel until his own retirement in 1968. Lloyd-Jones was considered to be the premier expository preacher of the post-World War II era. Toward the end of February 1981, he believed his earthly work was done. To his immediate family he said, "Don't pray for healing, don't try to hold me back from the glory," and on Sunday, March 1, 1981, D. Martyn Lloyd-Jones entered glory.

2　Charles Haddon Spurgeon (1834–1892). A noted British Baptist minister who, at age 20, became pastor of London's New Park Street Church (formerly pastored by John Gill), and which eventually moved to the newly built Metropolitan Tabernacle in 1861. Spurgeon frequently preached to audiences of 6,000–10,000 people (in days prior to electronic amplification), and was known as the Prince of Preachers. His 3,544 sermons have been published in a 63-volume collection. His popular daily devotions, "Morning and Evening" can be found on the Answers in Genesis website at: <<www.AnswersinGenesis.org/Devotions/devotions.asp>>

As I thought about Rob's years at college, I became even more perplexed about what had happened to him. He and his family sacrificed much so he could earn his theological degree. They moved to Sydney, a very expensive place to live in Australia. To keep expenses down, they rented a house that was part of a chicken farm on the outskirts of this great city. The first time I visited them I was somewhat shocked at the horrible smell from thousands and thousands of chickens. I'm not sure I could have put up with it.

Rob spent many hours a day traveling by train, bus, or car to attend college. He would do a lot of studying while sitting in the train. Rob and Brenda soon used up the money he had earned while at the bank. My wife and I were now in a position to support Rob and his family financially, as they had done for us.

Rob studied hard — long days and short nights. But he was a good student, and others also noted he was a great teacher of the Word of God. We gave Rob a complete set of Spurgeon's works as a graduation present. After he graduated, he talked to me about what he should do. He wanted to find a church where he could reach out to the community. He had a burden to reach Muslims and students for Christ. One of the things about Rob I'll never forget was his intense burden to preach the gospel of Christ. He just wanted to reach everyone he could with this message of salvation.

After considering a number of offers, he believed he was led to take up a position as pastor in a church on Australia's Gold Coast, one of the most pagan areas of Australia. I still remember the day he invited me along as he visited with the head deacon of this church. Rob was excited. He had a vision — not far from the church was a major university. He wanted to devise programs to reach the students. And he wanted to reach out to the community with the message of Christ. He saw such potential in this small church.

Rob threw his heart and soul into his work. He continued to study hard. He taught the Word of God verse by verse and applied it practically in today's world. Rob also had a special gift for playing the piano. After playing for the hymns and choruses, he would then get up and teach the Word of God. Brenda was deeply involved in the Sunday school and other outreaches. The church was growing. Some people who visited the Gold Coast for holidays heard that they could hear the Word of God taught uncompromisingly at Rob's church, so they would come and bring others. Rob's church also hosted the American tourists that my wife and I brought over each year for a special tour of Australia. Rob would have me preach, and the church would provide lunch for the tourists. What great memories.

But just when Rob's ministry was having great effect, and he was beginning to fulfill the vision and burden he had had for years, after all the sacrifice and "blood, sweat, and tears," and just as things seemed to be blessed and moving ahead — it all began to fall apart.

Like my distraught mother said, "I know God is in control. I know this is a sin-cursed world. I understand all that. But I still don't understand why this would happen to him — it doesn't seem to make sense — he worked so hard and preached so well. Why?"

During one of the many phone calls to my mother, she said in her grief, "It doesn't seem fair. He was such a man of God who loved and preached God's Word. There are all these people who compromise the Bible, and atheists who attack it. Why did this happen to such a person as Robert?"

I must admit that from a human perspective it doesn't seem fair. I could go over all the Bible verses with Mum about the sovereign God of the Bible being in control, that all things work together for good as the Bible states, that God's ways are higher than ours, and so on, but she knew all that. We were in the here and now, grieving over a situation that was hard to explain in the context of a loving God as described in the Bible.

If Rob had been killed in a traffic accident or contracted some deadly disease like cancer, it would have been a terrible shock, and many would have grieved greatly and probably asked many of the same questions. But to us it seemed much worse than that, since a great man of God had been stricken with a disease that caused him to lose his mind at a young age and die a slow death. He would leave behind a wife and two boys in those teenage formative years when fathers play such an important role in guiding their children to adulthood. The very gift of communication the Lord had given to him was taken away, and it was as if he was then put on the rack to be slowly tortured to death while family and friends were, if anything, tortured even more as the helpless spectators groping for answers.

During one of my earlier visits to Australia, before Rob had deteriorated too badly, I took him on a trip to a country town west of Brisbane. He couldn't talk much and some of his sentences didn't make sense. But he kept trying to tell me about his sermons, trying in some way to explain to me his love for preaching. He would say things like, "I did 14 on Genesis, and 10 on Romans and. . . ." I figured that he was telling me about the sermons he had preached on those books, but he couldn't say any more. His face contorted and he seemed perplexed. No matter how hard he tried to explain, he couldn't say it. His memory that was once so full of knowledge concerning God's Word was basically gone. It was such a distressing and pitiful scene.

At first, he could continue to play the piano and the piano accordion. We would motion to him to play and he would sit down at the piano or get out his accordion and play with a big smile on his face, with the same special talent the Lord had given him. Over time, though, this gift started to disappear. He could play fewer and fewer tunes, until he could play only parts of certain ones. Eventually all his wonderful abilities in this area ceased.

I'll never forget the time, after the disease had taken considerable control, when we took him to church knowing that he wouldn't understand (as far as we knew) what was happening. He could still appear to read (although we don't know what he understood), as he would pick up his favorite books, especially the Bible, and seemed to read the words, page after page. At this church service, we stood up to sing a hymn. Rob stood up and could still sing the words. He sang his heart out as my mother, tears running down her cheeks, watched with breaking heart. But at the end of the service, Rob did not seem to know anything about what was going on.

Why? And what about his wife, Brenda, and his two sons, Joshua and Geoffrey? How must they feel, knowing all that Rob did because of his love for God and His Word? How must they feel, watching him die, not just a "normal" death, but a slow, debilitating, utterly dehumanizing one? How must they have felt as they watched him being robbed of his ability to communicate and play the piano and accordion — the special gifts they all believed God had given him — as his mental faculties left him. Why?

How do I answer these questions? What do I say to Brenda and Joshua and Geoffrey? I'm a Christian, and I believe and love God's Word. I teach it all over the world. I preach the message of salvation and tell people about the wonderful God of love who created us, but how can I reconcile that with what happened with my brother Rob? What do I as the eldest child in our family say to my mother, my own wife and children, and my brothers and sisters, nieces, nephews, and so on? And what about the non-Christians who look on and see this Christian family struggling to cope with this terrible disaster in their lives — what do they think? What could we tell them in the midst of this tragedy that would cause them to look to the God of the Bible?

Are there any answers? How should I respond? Can I really reconcile this situation with the Christianity I am committed to? And what would Rob say if he understood the situation? How would he react? What would he say about the Bible and the God it portrays if he understood what had happened to him? Would he be angry? Would he turn his back on the Word of God he so faithfully preached? What would he say to God if he understood the nature of what had happened to him?

This has been a struggle for me and the whole family. No, there are no easy answers in one sense, but in my search for how I should respond as a Christian, I believe that light can be shed on this seemingly unfair, contradictory, and irreconcilable situation. After all, if the God of the Bible Rob believed in is real and His nature is as revealed in the pages of this revelation, then there has to be a way of reconciling what seems to us on a human level to be grossly unjust with a just and holy Creator — otherwise nothing makes sense.

Chapter 3

Pain, Plan, and Purpose

On the 9th of June, 1995, I was lying on a bed in an Indianapolis hotel room. The phone rang. It was my brother Robert calling me from the hospital in Brisbane, Australia, to tell me our father had just passed away. I was expecting the news, having spoken to Robert a number of times over the past few days. I had even had the opportunity, the day before, to speak to my father for the last time via cell phone while he lay in his hospital bed.

My family and I had by now been residing here in America for some years. My father and I had spoken a number of times concerning what I should do if he should die there in Australia while I was over here. He had told me that the most important thing for me to do was to continue preaching the Word of God he loved so much. I remember him saying, "If I die, there's no use coming back as I won't be here. You need to fulfill any of your speaking engagements — this is more important than coming back. Your priority has to be to preach the Word of God I taught you to love and trust."

As I put the phone down after hearing the sad news from Robert, it rang again. It was a Christian radio personality calling to interview me about the creation seminar I was to speak at that evening, commencing shortly. I carried out the interview, and then left the room to walk over to the convention center to speak to a large crowd of people. I think the only thing that kept me going was the fact that I didn't want to let my earthly father nor my Heavenly Father down. Fighting back tears and in an emotional turmoil, I prayed for strength and put my mind to the task of teaching the audience how important it was to trust God's infallible Word — from the beginning, from Genesis chapter 1.

Some time later, Robert told me of a fascinating conversation he had had with Dad. As Dad lay dying in hospital, Robert, who had been sitting with him, had asked him a question. "Dad, why did you have such a love for the Word of God? What was it that caused you to stand so strongly on God's Word?"

There's no doubt that my father loved the Bible. The picture I have even now of my father is of walking into the house and seeing him sitting in his favorite chair with his reading glasses on, a pen in his hand and his copiously marked Bible in his lap.

Dad was a teacher, and as a public school principal was transferred to many different towns around the State of Queensland. Dad and Mum started Sunday schools and ran Bible studies. They hosted missionaries and sponsored outreach programs to reach children and adults. In fact, it was at one of these programs in Innisfail (North Queensland) that I went forward at a meeting to make a commitment to be a missionary for the Lord.

Another image of my father was that he hated to knowingly compromise anything in the Bible and would always stand up for what he believed, regardless of the persecution he would receive. I vividly remember instances such as the time we were in church and the pastor preached about the account of the boy with the loaves and fishes, the feeding of the five thousand. The preacher made some comment to indicate that what happened wasn't really a miracle, but that because a little boy took out his loaves and fishes, he set a great example for the others to follow. My father was furious! At the end of the service, he led the whole family up to the pastor and began preaching to this man from the Bible to show clearly that what happened was a miracle. I remember him saying, "It is written," and he continued to expound the Bible's account of this event.

This sort of upbringing influenced the whole family, of course. I believe this is one of the major reasons Rob had such a love for the Word of God and wanted to work so hard to tell others about the gospel. Rob was also a "chip off the old block" as people say. He was like Dad in not wanting to compromise in any way, and wanting to stand up for what he believed was right, regardless of the consequences.

The question Rob had asked Dad was one I had never really asked him. As Rob told me about this, my heart started to race. This was important to me — I couldn't wait to hear the answer.

Rob then told me that Dad said that, when he was only 16 years old, his father had died. Because of this, as a young lad, Dad said that because he no longer had an earthly father to turn to, therefore he turned to his Heavenly Father and read His Word over and over again. As I listened, I became rather choked up. Yes, it made sense. Dad seemed to be always reading the Bible — he really loved God's Word.

I've recalled these events in my mind many times over the past years and certainly numerous times as I thought about what had happened to Rob. As I pondered these things in my heart, something became very clear to me — something that has been of great comfort in the midst of terrible sorrow.

When my father's father died, I'm sure those close to the situation would have grieved greatly. Maybe some may have even commented that it didn't seem fair that a young lad like my Dad would be left on this earth without his father. Maybe some might even have been angry at God, or perhaps some might have mocked Christians who believed in a holy, loving, and just God in the midst of such a situation.

However, many years later, we can look back and see a picture that probably no one would have even come close to guessing at the time. The situation that caused my father to turn to his Heavenly Father, and intimately get to know His Word, resulted in a godly family who stood on the authority of the Word of God. Rob became a preacher of the Word. I was instrumental in founding a ministry that has grown around the world. Others in the family have been involved in various Christian ministries. All of this put new meaning for me into the verse of Scripture many often quote when tragedy strikes, "For my thoughts are not your thoughts, neither are your ways my ways, says the LORD" (Isa. 55:8).

Who would have even thought that out of tragedy almost 60 years ago, a wonderful plan was executed that would result in literally millions hearing the truth of the Word of God — of which Rob had a special part? And there's no doubt in my mind that I would not be in this international ministry of *Answers in Genesis* (that reaches multi-thousands of people on a daily basis) if it weren't for my father's and mother's stand on the Word of God.

This sparked in my mind. Are there any examples in Scripture that might illustrate this as well?

Of course! The historical account of a very famous lady named Esther. In the Book of Esther in the Bible we read about King Ahasuerus and how he was displeased with the actions of his queen. Because of this, he began a search for a new queen — eventually choosing Esther, a beautiful young lady. The king was initially unaware that Esther was a Jewess, but as we read this fascinating event in the history of the Jews, we find out that all that happened to Esther resulted in the Jewish people being saved from annihilation.

Now consider what the Bible tells us concerning Esther:

> Now there was in the citadel of Susa a Jew of the tribe of Benjamin, named Mordecai son of Jair, the son of Shimei, the son of Kish, who had been carried into exile from Jerusalem by Nebuchadnezzar king of Babylon, among those taken captive with Jehoiachin king of Judah. Mordecai had a cousin named Hadassah, whom he had brought up because she had neither father nor mother. This girl, who was also known as Esther, was lovely in form and features, and Mordecai had taken her as his own daughter when her father and mother died (Esther 2:5–7).

We are not told of the events surrounding the death of Esther's parents. Perhaps they died of some horrible disease, or were tragically killed by an invading army. At the time of their death, some Jews might have questioned why God would allow a young girl to lose both her parents. Maybe even Mordecai questioned in his heart why God would allow such a seemingly terrible situation to befall such a lovely young girl as Esther.

Even though at the time no human being could foresee the future, God was working out a plan beyond what anyone could have imagined. Esther was being placed in circumstances such that she would be used by God to save the Jewish people.

Some time after Esther had become queen, a wicked man (Haman) attempted to have all Jews killed. Because Esther, as queen, had access to the king, she alone was in the position to petition the king to save the Jews. The Bible's account explains that, because of the laws of the land, for Esther to approach the king on this matter could end in her death.

Mordecai sent a message to Esther, urging her to petition the king. When she heard his request, she sent this reply: "All the king's officials and the people of the royal provinces know that for any man or woman who approaches the king in the inner court without being summoned the king has but one law: that he be put to death. The only exception to this is for the king to extend the gold scepter to him and spare his life. But thirty days have passed since I was called to go to the king" (Esther 4:9–11).

Esther obviously struggled with what she should do. When her words were reported to her cousin Mordecai, he said this to her:

> "Do not think that because you are in the king's house you alone of all the Jews will escape. For if you remain silent at this time, relief and deliverance for the Jews will arise from another place, but you and your father's family will perish. *And who knows but that you have come to royal position for such a time as this?*" (Esther 4:13–14, emphasis added).

Mordecai not only realized the powerful position Esther was in, but challenged Esther to think in terms of God's sovereign plan for her life. Could it be that all the circumstances of the past that had resulted in her being queen were planned by God just for this vital occasion? I'm sure Esther thought about her childhood and all that had happened to her. She stepped out in faith to save her people, and God worked in a wonderful way.

There is even much more to all of this, involving what at first would seem to be unrelated events surrounding the life of Mordecai. Circumstances caused the king to read a record of Mordecai's past actions, in which he had saved the king from an evil conspiracy to harm him. These events became entwined in a fascinating twist in the story of how this wicked man called Haman manipulated the king to try to eliminate the Jewish people. When the king found all this out, Haman ended up being sentenced to death.

I've often wondered about what was going through Mordecai's mind after the Jews were saved. I'm sure he pondered the past events surrounding his niece Esther. I wonder if he smiled as he realized the great plan of redemption that had come out of what must have seemed a great tragedy at the time. Perhaps he (and Esther) understood that the death of two people (Esther's parents) ultimately, through all the circumstances, led to the saving of an entire nation.

Besides, Esther's life and actions have been recorded and made a part of the Holy Word of God for eternity. How many millions and millions of times has the Book of Esther been read (and will continue to be read) to change hearts and lives? Few would have guessed that such a marvelous plan would come out of what at the time was no doubt a terrible tragedy, one that seemed grossly unfair from a human perspective.

To me, this correlates with my father's deathbed testimony to my brother Robert. As I contemplate the international outreach I am involved in, and the ministry Rob had during his short preaching ministry (as well as the ministry of others in our family), one could ask the question, "Who would have thought that a young teenager's father's death would produce circumstances that two generations later would lead to millions hearing about God's infallible authoritative Word and the gospel?"

Even though it doesn't stop the grief, and I must admit I still heave a sigh and shake my head in disbelief, it has been a great comfort to me to be reminded that God is also working in the circumstances surrounding Rob. "And we know that in all things God works for the good of those who love him, who have been called according to his purpose" (Rom. 8:28). Maybe something even greater than Esther's situation could come out of this — who knows? After all, I would never have written this half of this book if it weren't for what has happened to Rob. And who knows how many people will eventually read this publication? Who knows how many lives will be positively affected for the Lord? Who knows how people around the world may be challenged as a result of these pages? How many other grieving people may be comforted by this testimony that has now been put into print for the world to read?

Chapter 4

A Voice from the Past

What would Rob himself say if he were able to understand all that has happened and was asked to respond?

A year or so before he was stricken with this terrible disease, Rob excitedly told me about a Bible study program, produced by a well-known Australian theological college, that he was using at church. He so wanted to teach people God's Word. However, he was immensely saddened to find that this program compromised the Word of God in the Book of Genesis with evolutionary teaching.

Rob understood that the history in Genesis is foundational to the rest of the Bible. All Christian doctrine is founded in this history. He also understood that Genesis makes it plain that there was no death, bloodshed, or disease before sin.

It was the sin of the first man, Adam, that resulted in the judgment of death and the entrance of disease, suffering, and violence into the world. Because Adam and Eve and the animals were vegetarian before sin (as recorded in Genesis

1:29–30), Rob understood that one could not accommodate millions of years and/or evolutionary teaching into the Bible, as this Bible study program did. To do so would be to admit that the Bible's words cannot be trusted and God would be an ogre. This is because integral to the notion of millions of years is the idea that the fossil record (with its evidence of death, disease, suffering, and violence) was laid down millions of years before man came on the scene. Now at the end of the sixth day of creation, after finishing the creation of all living things and Adam and Eve, God described the creation as "very good" (Gen. 1:31). As Rob said to me, "If God said death, suffering, disease, and violence is very good, then God is an ogre. No, God created a perfect creation that has been corrupted by sin. There is no way the billions of fossils could have been laid down before man. I believe you're right in saying that most of the fossils resulted from the flood of Noah's day."

The Genesis section of this Bible study program was extremely upsetting to Rob. He saw what this theological college had done as an attack on God's Word — and, like our father, Rob hated compromise. He realized that if one could take man's fallible interpretation of the world and reinterpret the Bible accordingly in Genesis, then this could be done with any passage in the Bible. People could start questioning the Resurrection or the Virgin Birth — after all, no scientist has seen anyone rise from the dead, so maybe this part of the Bible should be reinterpreted also! Most liberal theological colleges reason just like that, yet they started out as evangelical a few generations ago.

Rob was a defender of the faith. He was so convicted by this turn of events that he wrote to the president of the college responsible for this program. Eventually he visited this president and challenged him personally concerning this matter.

I want you to read Rob's own words dealing with this issue, as this will help us answer the question as to what Rob would have said about his condition if he could:

> If death came into this world as a result of Adam's sin, where is there place for the evolutionary process? The evolutionary process is a process of death and struggle. If we were simply guided by the Bible with no other influence, I have no doubt that the only conclusion that could be made would be that death came into the world as a result of sin. . . .
>
> Obviously, we do not have all the answers in respect to the original creation, and certain questions remain as a result of the Fall. However, we must acknowledge that we are looking back at a perfect creation through fallen eyes, and our first and authoritative revelation must come from the words of Scripture.
>
> So many people . . . do not approach the creation doctrine from Scripture first, but allow theories and assumptions from certain fields of science to create a framework of thinking that is then taken to Scripture, instead of the other way around.

Rob's own words tell me that if he understood his situation and was asked to respond, he would go immediately to the Bible, beginning with Genesis, and answer from there. I have no doubt he would expound the Book of Genesis and help people to understand that a once-perfect creation, described by God as "very good," has been marred by sin. Without the literal history in Genesis, Rob would not have a consistent, logical answer.

Rob would explain that he, like everyone else, had been given a death sentence at the point of conception, because all people are descendants of the first man, Adam. Actually, when Adam sinned, we were all "in" Adam, and thus must suffer the consequences of his rebellious action against a Holy God. And of course we have all individually, personally taken part in that rebellion in our own lives, too.

Even though I was fairly sure I knew what Robert would say, I wanted so much to be able to communicate with him and hear his answers. I was sure he wouldn't, overall, be angry but would explain from the Bible that none of us really even has the right to live. Rob understood the sovereignty of God, and I'm sure he would tenderly explain this to my mother. He was a gentle soul who was very caring with people. He would react like our father, saying, "It is written."

During my lifetime, I've heard non-Christians mock God when they see a Christian suffering by saying such things as, "That person doesn't deserve to suffer like that. How can a God of love let someone who serves Him go through such a terrible situation?"

Does Rob deserve to suffer the way he is now? When you think about it from a Christian perspective, we all deserve much, much more than the suffering afflicting Rob. You see, because of our rebellious condition, we don't even deserve to live. But God didn't annihilate us, he has allowed us to live — while at the same time giving us a taste of what life is like without God. Everything around us, as well as our bodies, falls apart. This is a necessary consequence of rebellion against our Creator. But God in His grace and mercy comforts us in our affliction, and has provided a way for us to return to a perfect relationship with Him. We don't deserve what God has done for us. We don't deserve even the life we do have.

As I returned to my room after visiting the nursing home, my youngest brother Stephen gave me an audio tape of one of Robert's sermons, entitled "The Experience Trap — Healing," that Rob preached on June 1, 1997 — only a couple of years before his major health issue began to manifest itself. "You've got to hear this," he said, "Rob deals directly with the very issue he's being confronted with right now. It's almost prophetic."

I couldn't wait to hear the tape. What did he say that relates to this current situation? Did he have some insight I hadn't been given that could throw more light on the situation? Could his words help his family, and others who are grieving over the pain and suffering of a loved one, understand how to cope with his present condition?

I eagerly devoured every word spoken by Rob in this sermon. It was very illuminating and extremely thought-provoking. It was as if God had been preparing Rob and his family and friends for what was coming.

Regarding the origin of sickness, he stated, "You see, if there was no sin in the world . . . there wouldn't be any sickness and there would be no death." This, of course, is totally in accord with what he had written to the Bible college president as discussed earlier.

So Rob understood that the reason for sickness is because of the fall of man as recorded in Genesis. But what about the accusation people sometimes make that sickness must be the result of some specific sin in a person's life?

Well, Rob explained that the consequences of certain sins (such as alcohol abuse, homosexual behavior, and so on) could lead to sickness. Also, there are times when God can cause people to become sick because of their rebellion against Him. Rob discussed this issue when dealing with James chapter 5, in which the word is actually "weakness" (*asthenei*). This is connected to the word *kamnonta*, meaning "weary person," to refer to the sick one, and as such usually refers to sickness in a *spiritual* sense. However, he also went on to say:

> But of course there are other people as well, who have some dreadful sicknesses, some dreadful diseases, that inflict them. And yet friends, it's not because of any specific sin in their life, nothing to do with any specific sin in their life at all. And so we need to understand that balance . . . sin has been in the world since Adam and Eve rebelled. It is called "original sin," and from there of course, sin has been the thing that has been really damaging every single person.

Rob goes on to point out that (apart from those alive at His return) "there is not a person in this world who will not die [before] the Lord Jesus comes again. . . ." Here he reminds people that the ultimate "sickness" that we all have to face, as a result of sin, is death.

Okay, Rob understood why there is sickness and death in this world — a result of Adam's rebellion in the Garden of Eden. Because we are all descendants of Adam, the Bible tells us that we sinned in Adam. Thus, we all suffer the same problem.

But though Rob was, yes, a sinner, he was also a man of God. Not only had he trusted the Lord Jesus Christ, the Creator of the universe, for salvation, he had also dedicated his life to preaching God's Word. Even though he, like everyone else, was under the condemnation of death, surely a God of love wouldn't let some terrible disease inflict a person like Rob? And even if he contracted some horrible disease, wouldn't (couldn't) the all-powerful God of the Bible heal him anyway? Well, as we know, Rob did become afflicted with a disease most of us don't even want to think about — a disease that causes one to lose one's mind and die slowly.

Sometimes, when I called my mother to see how Rob was doing, she would tell me how she'd been up all night praying that God would heal him. "I believe God can heal him," she would say, "don't you believe that?"

Yes, I believed God could heal Rob. God can do anything. And there have been real accounts from people (like that of my friend and colleague Dr. Carl Wieland which you read about in the first half) who can testify to God's miraculous healing in their life — though not necessarily in the way we might have wanted.

I praise the Lord for the faith my mother showed in this. She has pleaded and pleaded in tears with the Lord to intervene for Rob. And I praise the Lord even more that, even though Rob's condition continued to worsen, my mother's faith and trust in God did not wane but grew. She recognized that God was in total control of the situation and that He heard the prayers of a grieving mother.

In his sermon, Rob addressed the issue of healing. As you consider what he stated, you will see his sincere devotion to the Lord and his intense burden to challenge people to focus on Him and Him only:

> In many churches today, the focus is on our ailments, on our illnesses and on our sicknesses, and so on. But the problem is that when that is the

focus . . . we are focusing on ourselves rather than focusing on the Lord Jesus Christ, rather than focusing on what the Bible is actually saying and telling us.

Now you see, I am not for a moment suggesting that the Lord can't heal and the Lord can't bring miraculous things in people's lives, I am not suggesting that for a moment.

At this point in his sermon, he recounted the testimony of Dr. Carl Wieland that you read about in the first half.

Rob was obviously explaining that God *can* heal, but the focus should never be on ourselves — our focus should always be on the Lord Jesus Christ. So what did Rob mean by this?

He indicates that nowhere in the Bible will we find that we can demand healing and miraculous signs from the Lord. He says:

> The miraculous sign that the Lord gives us in fact, and the sign that we constantly need to be seeking and focusing on, is the sign where the Lord Jesus came into this world and gave His life up and shed His blood that you and I could be drawn to Christ. Where He rose from the dead, this is the greatest sign in the history of this world, and it will be the greatest sign until the Lord Jesus comes again. That Christ came into the world to give His life [see. Matt. 12:38–42].

The day I went through Rob's sermon word by word, I sat beside his bed in the nursing home holding his feeble hand, thinking about these things, and mulling over in my mind this next statement from further on in his sermon. You see, as I looked at his weakened body and his blank, now somewhat sunken face that once was filled with joy reflecting his Christian character, I kept thinking, *This is not normal, Rob. Surely this is not normal for this to happen to such a one as you.*

Now read Rob's statement, as if he foresaw what was going to happen. Referring to Paul and his thorn in the flesh, Rob states:

> I am going to say this twice . . . I would like this to melt into your mind and into your heart. I want it to be written indelibly on your mind so that it will never, ever be wiped away. Please understand this. You see the apostle Paul when we look at the whole New Testament . . . Paul saw illness and he saw sickness as normal (N-O-R-M-A-L). I'd like to underline it with a great big felt pen and write it indelibly in every one of our minds. The apostle Paul saw sickness and illness as normal living in a world ruined by sin. I'll say it again; the apostle Paul saw illness and sickness as normal living in a world that has been ruined by sin.

If Rob was able to look on at this disease-racked body, I thought, knowing the person lying there was a devout Christian, he would say, through tears of compassion, that this is the sort of thing to be expected in a sin-cursed universe. Although it is abnormal in the sense of not being the way things should have been, were it not for sin — it should be considered "normal" in that sense, in this fallen world. I believe Rob would then tell us that instead of focusing on the disease, we need to focus on Christ.

In fact, I'm sure Rob would say if he could, "I know it's sad watching my body die and not being able to communicate with me. I know you feel a horrible separation, but look at what the Bible says. It doesn't promise we will be physically healed in this sin-cursed world. Remember, we are all sick and dying because of sin — this is to be considered normal in this world. The people who were healed or raised from the dead by Christ during His earthly ministry, or through the Apostles, only had a temporary reprieve. Eventually, they had to die anyway. They could not escape this normal course of events for this world. But, for the Christian, the wonderful news is that God does promise to comfort us and strengthen us, knowing we are sinful creatures living in such a fallen world."

As Rob said in his sermon, quoting J.I. Packer, "The ultimate reason from our standpoint why God fills our lives with troubles and perplexities of one sort and another, it is to ensure that we shall learn to hold him fast." Rob then sums up the point he makes over and over again in this presentation:

> The reason why the Bible spends so much of its time reiterating that God is a strong rock, a firm defense and a sure refuge and help for the weak, is that God spends so much of His time bringing home to us that we are weak, both mentally and morally, and dare not trust ourselves to find or to follow the right road. God wants us to feel that our way through life is rough and perplexing so that we may learn to lean on Him. Therefore He takes steps to drive us out of self-confidence, to trust in himself.

I'm sure Rob had passages in mind concerning Paul, like 2 Corinthians 1:3–11:

> Praise be to the God and Father of our Lord Jesus Christ, the Father of compassion and the God of all comfort, who comforts us in all our troubles, so that we can comfort those in any trouble with the comfort we ourselves have received from God. For just as the sufferings of Christ flow over into our lives, so also through Christ our comfort overflows. If we are distressed, it is for your comfort and salvation; if we are comforted, it is for your comfort, which produces in you patient endurance of the same sufferings we suffer. And our hope for you is firm, because we know that just as you share in our sufferings, so also you share in our comfort.
>
> We do not want you to be uninformed, brothers, about the hardships we suffered in the province of Asia. We were under great pressure, far beyond our ability to endure, so that we despaired even of life. Indeed, in our hearts we felt the sentence of death. But this happened that we might not rely on ourselves but on God, who raises the dead. He has delivered us from such a deadly peril, and he will deliver us. On him we have set our hope that he will continue to deliver us, as you help us by your prayers. Then many will give thanks on our behalf for the gracious favor granted us in answer to the prayers of many.

Rob wanted people to understand that God teaches us, through Paul, that even though we have to live with the consequences of sin in this physical universe, nonetheless, God loves us so much that he will provide the comfort necessary for us to cope with the various situations in which we find ourselves.

Paul, of all people, learned this lesson. Rob compared Job to Paul to instruct us in this matter:

> Job was afflicted, where the Lord allowed the devil to afflict Job . . . and there the Lord allowed the devil to afflict Paul . . . and whatever this thorn was, and by the way, the word is really that he was "buffeted" and it means "a fist crushing bones." It means this, that whatever Paul had it was incredibly painful. I don't know what it was, whether it was his eye, or whatever it be, it was incredibly painful.
>
> Now 2 Corinthians 12:8 [states] "three times I pleaded with the Lord to take it away from me." Three times he asked the Lord to take it away. But it didn't happen. It didn't go, so the question you see that I must ask, the question I have to ask the apostle Paul is this: Paul, you didn't have enough faith. That must be the whole answer, Paul. You didn't work up enough faith. You didn't believe enough, that is your problem. So many people face exactly that sort of aspect today. So many people. By the way, I want you to notice that Paul [in this situation], nowhere does he bind the devil, nowhere does he rebuke, nowhere does he cast this out, nowhere! Verses 9 and 10 [state], "But He said to me, my grace is sufficient for you, for my power is made perfect in weakness. Therefore I will boast all the more

gladly about my weaknesses so that Christ's power may rest on me. That is why for Christ's sake I delight in weaknesses, in insults, in hardships, in persecutions, in difficulties, for when I am weak then I am strong." You see, what he found is his need to trust in the Lord Jesus Christ, to rest there.

Chapter 5

Ultimate Recovery

As Rob's wife and boys, my mother, and my other brothers and sisters sit by his bed, from our human perspective, we want so much to see Rob restored. But if he could speak, I know he would tell us that he is restored — he is healed, from the worst disease — sin.

It is true that when Christ was on earth, He carried out great miracles, including wonderful healings of sick people, but it's also true, as Rob preached, that "when the Lord Jesus came, His whole purpose and the reason why He came . . . [was] to pay the penalty for our sin, to [appease] the wrath of God, and to rise again from the dead. And you see, His whole purpose was so that He would make us what He intends us to be. What does He intend us to be? Well, you see, He is speaking there about freedom for the prisoners, sight for the blind, release of the oppressed. . . . It means this, He paid for our sins, He brought us forgiveness. That's what it's all about, real and genuine forgiveness so that He would bring us into a right relationship with God, with the Lord Jesus Christ."

Rob explains that the record we have of Christ's ministry shows He can overcome the effects of the Curse. He illustrates this through various miracles. But this is a lesson to give us a hint of what the new heavens and earth will be like where there will be no Curse. In this present sin-cursed world, we live in sin-ravaged bodies that cause us to groan. But what an encouragement to know that Christ will one day restore our bodies, and the whole creation, to perfection! How exciting it is to see a glimpse of this through the ministry of Christ and the Apostles. Of course, we wish this would happen now — and at times, for His purposes, God does ordain specific miraculous events to overcome the consequences of the Curse. But at the right time, God will bring this present era to a close, and then for all those who do trust in Him, we will have that final healing.

Rob continues in his sermon:

> In fact, we know that in the Gospels we see that the Lord Jesus went out and He went out healing people. He went out casting out evil spirits, He went out raising people from the dead, He did that. He stopped the storm, didn't He? Remember that? Now you see in all of this what the Lord Jesus is showing us is our restoration is to be spiritual. That's what He is talking about, that's what He is showing us. That our restoration is spiritual now. Right now. You see, right now, you and I through the Lord Jesus Christ are spiritually restored to God. Right now, through the Lord Jesus, through His death and His resurrection. But you see it is now and not yet. It is yet to come.

. . . We are living in a world where we are living now and not yet. Now we are spiritually restored to God, spiritually restored through the Lord Jesus Christ, yes, but it is yet to come. What is yet to come? Well, you see this is the whole perspective of all this that I have been reading and what the Lord Jesus came into this world for. You see, what is yet to come is a new heaven and a new earth, that we are looking forward to. And in fact that is where our focus needs to be, friends. Because in the new heaven and the new earth the Lord Jesus, who *is* righteousness, will dwell there, and we shall dwell with Him. Isn't that fantastic? In the new heaven and the new earth. We don't want to focus on this world, it's a world ruined by sin. We don't want to focus on ourselves, we are people who have been ruined by sin, we want to focus on the new heaven and the new earth that is yet to come. And in that new heaven and the new earth, friends, we're now fully restored to Christ, yet to come, here in that new heaven and new earth, there will be no sickness. There will be no disease, there will be no demons, there will be no death, there will be no chaos . . . [Rev. 21:4, 22:3].

Everything is going to be peaceful and perfect. Wonderful, isn't it? You see now and not yet. Restored to Christ today, yes, and yet to come. All that we are looking forward to. In fact, you see the New Testament emphasis is not primarily on physical healing, but it is on the power of the Holy Spirit who brings us into a right relationship with the Lord Jesus Christ.

That is the primary aspect of the New Testament.

Rob then explains this further by expounding the passage in Isaiah 53:5:

> But he was wounded for our transgressions, he was bruised for our iniquities: the chastisement of our peace was upon him; and with his stripes we are healed.

Rob explains that Peter, in 1 Peter 2:22–24, quotes from, and gives us the correct understanding of, this Isaiah passage. Peter states: " 'He committed no sin, and no deceit was found in his mouth.' When they hurled their insults at him, he did not retaliate; when he suffered, he made no threats. Instead, he entrusted himself to him who judges justly. He himself bore our sins in his body on the tree, so that we might die to sins and live for righteousness; by his wounds you have been healed."

Rob's sermon continues:

> What's the context here? That's what we have to examine. Let's put the Bible back in context, because this is what a lot of people do, they take verses out of context and they will just apply them to whatever they want. But the context here is this — that Peter is talking about the death of the Lord Jesus Christ for our sins. That's the whole emphasis and that's what he gets out of Isaiah 53. In fact, this aspect here that says "and by His wounds you have been healed," the Greek terminology here, "you have been

healed," it's in what we call the passive sense [voice]. . . . It means you have *already* been healed.[1]

Friends, you are all healed, because, you see, what the Bible is telling us is if you are in the Lord Jesus Christ, Christ died to shed His blood so that you can be washed clean from your sin. That's the whole perspective of it. That's what it means. That's the context of it all. You *already have* been healed. You *already have* been washed clean from your sin. You have been restored to Christ, and it's now and not yet, yet to come, see? Yet to come when we will have the new heaven and new earth and then there will be no sicknesses and so on, but the primary emphasis is definitely not on physical healing. Our primary focus here is on the Lord Jesus Christ and His death and resurrection for us. That's what that verse means.

As I sat beside Rob's bed watching my mother lovingly caress his head, she said, "I wish he could just say 'Mum' one more time." Instead there were times when her son, obviously not knowing what he was doing, would push her

---

1 Note that the physical healing which Jesus brought to people in Matthew 8 is there said to be a fulfilment of the Isaiah 53:5 prophecy. It has been argued that this in itself indicates that the meaning cannot be stretched to a blanket promise to heal all Christians today of everything. The typological link seems unmistakeable. Physical disease, one of the results of sin via the Curse, being dealt with as a foretaste of Christ's dealing with the root cause on the Cross. It is the Cross which will in due course lead to the elimination altogether of death, the "last enemy" (1 Cor. 15:26).

away — seemingly to reject the loving hand that was caressing his forehead — the loving mother that was patiently feeding him his favorite drinks to help satisfy his hunger and hopefully give him some joy and comfort — if he could even experience such feelings in his embattled state.

I looked on with mixed emotion. On the one hand, I found it hard to hold back the tears. On the other hand, I rejoiced that Rob already had the most important healing of all — the spiritual healing that meant when he passed away from this earth, he would be totally healed for eternity.

As I thought about this, the Bible verse that came to mind was Romans 8:18, where Paul, who suffered greatly in many ways, says, "For I reckon that the sufferings of this present time are not worthy to be compared with the glory which shall be revealed in us."

The Bible tells us something that science knows very well. "The length of our days is seventy years — or eighty, if we have the strength; yet their span is but trouble and sorrow, for they quickly pass, and we fly away" (Ps. 90:10).

We consider someone who lives to 80 years old to have had a long life. However, contemplate this — how long is 80 compared to eternity? As Job stated in Job 8:9, "We were born only yesterday and know nothing, and our days on earth are but a shadow."

Even though we live in time, and to us the sufferings of a loved one like Rob seem so prolonged, compared to eternity it's not even a fleeting moment. Now that doesn't in any way negate the trauma of it all in this life, but we do need to put it all in perspective and try to see more of the "big picture" as God sees it.

I'm sure Rob might say to us, "Look, I'm spiritually healed and that's all that matters. Everyone (unless the Lord returns during their lifetime) is going to die of something. Some people get heart disease; some have kidney disease; some get cancer; I just happen to have a brain disease. This is not abnormal in this fallen world; this is all normal. Don't despair for me. Rejoice that I have the healing, that I can look forward to an eternity with the Lord and all those fellow humans who also have this spiritual healing the Lord Jesus Christ offers us. Remember what Paul tells us in 2 Corinthians 4:17, "For our light and momentary troubles are achieving for us an eternal glory that far outweighs them all."

Chapter 6

Dust and Ashes —— the Key to True Hope

I must say I often wonder how a non-Christian can even begin to cope in situations like the one our family has found itself in. For such a person, this life, as far as they believe, is all there is. When a loved one dies, they believe that is the end of them — they exist no more. How they must despair.

But surely, it must even be more despairing to think that if this life is all there is, then compared to time itself, the few years they live are meaningless. They die, and won't even remember they were ever alive — what's the point of living, anyhow? What's the point of putting your trust in material goods and having a good time if at some point such a person won't even know they existed? No wonder Paul says, in 1 Thessalonians 4:13, "Brothers, we do not want you to be ignorant about those who fall asleep, or to grieve like the rest of men, who have no hope."

Personally, I think that, even though we all see people dying around us every day, many people (especially non-

Christians) have, in a sense, at some level of their consciousness, convinced themselves that this will not happen to them. In a way, they try to avoid reality in order to somehow think that they can get out of dealing with death. But when someone close to them dies, or there is a major tragedy like the destruction of the World Trade Center in New York in 2001, they don't know how to deal with it. They sorrow for a while until they can shelve the issue again and get on with life.

However, a Christian does not sorrow as the world does, because we can rejoice in knowing that when someone like my brother Rob dies, he will be totally healed and living with his Creator for ever. Now, this is not to say that we shouldn't pray for physical healing for Rob in this earthly life. Even Rob, as previously quoted, acknowledged that God can, and at times does for His purposes, bring such healing. However, it is certainly not the normal course of events in today's world — the "normal" course of events, as Rob has clearly stated, is that people suffer all sorts of trauma in their fallen state. Even if God heals someone physically, eventually they still will have to succumb to the effects of sin and the Curse on their physical body.

In his sermon, Rob went on to say what he believed the priority should be in dealing with someone who is sick. Without in any way negating the fact that we pray for physical healing, Rob challenged his congregation this way:

> I suggest that when we are talking to somebody who is sick, that we need to restructure our terminology, that we might go to the person and say, "Brother, sister, I want you to know that we

love you dearly. I want you to know we can see how much you are sick, and we are really praying to the Lord for you. We are just praying for you, really praying. And we want you to know how much we want to help you, and we want to come and help you. I'd like to pray with you. We are going to bring some meals for your family. We want to help you."

In other words, Rob recognized that as sickness is a normal part of this life (even though we can ask God for healing), we need to encourage the sick person by telling them that we love them and are praying for them and will be helping this person's family with meals and in other ways will want to share in the burden of this tribulation. Our prayers would include asking God to help comfort all those involved, as He has promised to do.

For this particular visit to Australia, I flew over especially to spend time with my mother and Brenda, the boys, and the rest of the family, just to encourage them and share their burden during this time. Family and friends have extended helping hands in all sorts of ways to Brenda, Joshua, and Geoffrey. We want them to know that we love them and will help to provide for them during and after this difficult time they are going through.

Sadly, I have found that because of Robert's particular disease which involved him losing considerable self-awareness and his ability to communicate etc., many people, including many Christians, don't know how to handle the situation. For many, I believe it is because they don't have a full understanding like Rob did of the sin-cursed nature of this world, and how we should view life through God's "eyes." So they don't know how to cope with a man of God like Rob being in such a terrible physical condition. Some have even cruelly suggested that there has been lack of faith and that's why Robert has not been healed.

In 2 Timothy 4:20, we read, "Erastus stayed in Corinth, and I left Trophimus sick in Miletus." I'm sure Paul prayed for Trophimus. However, Paul also recognized that sickness is a "normal" part of this life. No one is condemned here for a lack of faith causing this man's sickness. The same Paul through whom God at other times had miraculously healed the lame — even raised the dead — left Trophimus knowing that, under the sovereignty of God, his ministry would not in any way be thwarted.

In the passage in 2 Corinthians 1:8, quoted earlier, we read that Paul even says, "We despaired even of life." Paul knew toward the end of his life that he would be martyred. Certainly, God could have stopped this, and no doubt Paul prayed concerning this matter, but he also recognized that in a world where "men loved darkness instead of light," (John 3:19) this also was a "normal" course of events. Besides which, the sovereign God of the Bible would work all these things for good anyway.

I believe that if Rob could speak to us, he would remind us of those great people of faith in Hebrews 11, of which some "faced jeers and flogging, while still others were chained and put in prison. They were stoned; they were sawed in two; they were put to death by the sword. They went about in sheepskins and goatskins, destitute, persecuted and mistreated" (Heb. 11:36–37). Rob, in the normal course of events in this world, has been allowed to suffer a terrible disease.

As Rob said in this sermon, "You know that we must realize that Job's suffering was part of God's plan. That's what it was. It must also be true for many people today who suffer so badly, and through it all, you see Job learned the necessity of submitting to the Lord's sovereign purpose, no matter what the cost might be."

Of course, that does not mean that we shouldn't seek medical help, and should just "resign" ourselves to sickness. This is a position Rob never took. The Bible makes it clear, including through the actions of Christ himself, that local, temporary efforts to alleviate the Curse, such as healing of sicknesses, binding up wounds, and so on, are to be encouraged.

As I said earlier, look at the wonderful plan God had worked out, in the midst of tragedy, that resulted in Esther saving the Jewish nation. Sometimes God has asked people to sacrifice greatly so that His sovereign purposes of redemption and necessary judgment could be carried out. Imagine if you were Ezekiel, and were told that for God's purposes for the Jews, your wife, whom you loved so much, was going to be taken away from you, and you were not allowed to grieve.

> Son of man, with one blow I am about to take away from you the delight of your eyes. Yet do not lament or weep or shed any tears (Ezek. 24:16).

And think about Job's suffering, to which Rob refers in his sermon. I doubt Job realized that a book would be written outlining all the details of what happened to him, to be incorporated into the holy, written Word of God to teach generation after generation necessary truths that God wanted us to understand.

I often quote the Book of Job in my talks on Genesis. I refer to Job 40:15 to explain that the animal God described to Job to remind him of God's greatness could well have been a dinosaur. Thousands of children and adults have benefited from such teaching. In fact, one of my favorite verses of the Bible is found in Job 38:4, "Where were you when I laid the earth's foundation? Tell me, if you understand." I teach children (and adults) all over the world to remember to ask the question God, in effect, asked Job when they hear someone talk about millions of years — "Were you there?" I have heard so many testimonies from parents who say this helped their children combat the false teaching of millions of years. Many have told of instances where children have asked evolutionary scientists, "Were you there?" and then observed them lost for words.

But you know one of the most important things we learn from the Book of Job? As we read chapters 38 through 41, we find God asks Job a series of questions. Do you know this, Job? What about this? God uses example after example to finally bring Job to the point in Job 42 where we read:

> Then Job replied to the LORD: "I know that you can do all things; no plan of yours can be thwarted. You asked, 'Who is this that obscures my counsel without knowledge?' Surely I spoke of things I did not understand, things too wonderful for me to know. You said, 'Listen now, and I will speak; I will question you, and you shall answer me.' My ears had heard of you but now my eyes have seen you. Therefore I despise myself and repent in dust and ashes" (Job 42:1–6).

Basically, this is the answer to the issue of death and suffering. Job acknowledged that compared to what God knows, he knew nothing. He repented of his human arrogance and totally submitted his life to the all-knowing sovereign God of the universe. Job learned the lesson we read about in Isaiah 55:9: "As the heavens are higher than the earth, so are my ways higher than your ways and my thoughts than your thoughts."

Chapter 7

Reality and Comfort in a Dying World

So what have I learned through this sad ordeal concerning my brother Robert? I have been reminded of many things:

1. Life is short — compared to eternity, it is not even a fleeting moment. All people need to face the fact that they will die and must be ready to deal with this.
2. The most important thing for every human being is that we are spiritually healed — this is so much more important than physical healing of a body for which death/sickness is inevitable anyway, because of the Genesis curse. We must get our priorities right in accordance with Scripture.
3. We need to trust God in all circumstances, no matter how tragic they seem at the time.
4. God's thoughts are so far above ours, we can't even begin to imagine them.

5. God does work all things for good, even though we may not see it at the time.
6. We need to try to see things more from a "big picture" perspective and not just focus on ourselves and the situations we may be in.

The bottom line in all of this is that we are not going to have all the answers as to why things like Rob's sickness have been allowed to happen. Only God knows everything — we are just fallible human beings who, like Job, need to recognize that we know nothing compared to what God knows.

Even though I give lots of lectures on the topic of creation and evolution, I explain to people that no one can scientifically prove creation or Noah's flood (or evolution and millions of years, for that matter), as none of us were there to witness these events. However, the Bible's account of origins in Genesis does make sense of the evidence in the world around us, and observational science confirms the biblical record. For instance, Genesis tells us that God created distinct kinds of animals and plants to reproduce after their own kinds. The science of genetics confirms that no new genetic information is produced from matter, and animals and plants reproduce their own kind — even though there can be great variation (even speciation) within a kind because of the variety in the genes.

Now none of this scientifically proves the Bible's account of creation — but real observational science certainly agrees with the model built upon the Bible (not evolution), and thus confirms its accuracy. We could do this with many different examples, including Noah's flood and fossils and so on.

However, ultimately, as we read in Hebrews 11:6, "Without faith it is impossible." There will always be a faith aspect, since no human being has always been there and no human being knows everything. Only the God of the Bible is omniscient, omnipotent, and omnipresent.

This has greatly helped me in dealing with the issue of death and suffering. God's Word tells us clearly where death and sickness originated. We understand we live in a fallen world. Each of us needs to recognize that we are sinful creatures living under a curse because of sin. Death for every human being is inevitable ("Just as man is destined to die once, and after that to face judgment" — Hebrews 9:27). Every person needs to be spiritually healed. Total healing doesn't come until we leave this sin-cursed universe. God has a sovereign plan far greater than we could imagine. We don't know everything — in fact, we know nothing compared to God.

Thus, we need to put our faith and trust in God's Word and the fact that He is in total control. I realize it's hard to do in the midst of a tragedy that we are a part of — but nonetheless, we all need to come to the place Job arrived at:

> I know that you can do all things; no plan of yours can be thwarted . . . therefore I despise myself and repent in dust and ashes.

And the words in 1 Samuel 3:18, "So Samuel told him everything, hiding nothing from him. Then Eli said, 'He is the LORD; let him do what is good in his eyes.'"

Yes, it is the Lord, let Him do what is good in His eyes.

At the end of my final visit to the nursing home for this trip to Australia, knowing that this could be my final goodbye to Robert, I bent over and kissed him on his forehead, "Goodbye, Robert. I love you, brother." I left the room somewhat choked up but with a real peace that came over me knowing he was the Lord's and in the Lord's hand. I weep, but not as others who don't have this wonderful sure hope of eternal life.

As I left the nursing home with my mother, we went next door to the retirement village to visit a dear friend, Effie. She was one of the first secretaries for the creation ministry in its early days. Her godly husband, Jack, had recently died after a painful bout with cancer.

Effie was hurting, struggling to cope with the complexities of living in this world — dealing with bank accounts, her husband's will and so on. She talked about Jack and what a loss it was. My mother talked about how she has been coping in the years since Dad died. She explained how it was only her trust in, and strength from, the Lord that enabled her to cope.

I looked on as two widows comforted each other and shared one another's burdens. The separation they felt from their husbands, and the separation we also felt from Robert (even though his body was still with us), reminded me once again of the awfulness of sin. We grieve over this separation. How much must God grieve over the separation between us and Him because of our sin! What a reminder that we need spiritual healing. And what an indescribable blessing to know that God himself provided all that is needed for this healing — even though we have done nothing to deserve it.

Yes, it's a sin-cursed universe — an abnormal state from God's viewpoint, which will not last. How I praised God for the comfort He was to these two hurting women.

As I walked back to the car with my mother, I thought about the fact that one day I'll have to say goodbye to her also.

Yes, sickness, suffering and death is a normal part of this life. But:

Praise be to the God and Father of our Lord Jesus Christ, the Father of compassion and the God of all comfort (2 Cor. 1:3).

Therefore encourage [comfort] each other with these words (1 Thess. 4:18).

As we drove away, my mother told me how she had felt when she walked out of the hospital after my father died. She said she looked around at all the people going to and fro and said to herself, "They don't care, they just don't care."

As I looked around, I saw people going about their daily business, boarding buses, coming out of stores with armloads of goods, children laughing on their way home from school — people going to and fro, not caring about what was happening to my brother Robert. But why should they, they didn't know him or know what was happening to him. Why should they care? But as I looked at them I thought of the fact that each one of them is, like Rob, going to face death one day. Many of them will end up in nursing homes, aimlessly staring at the wall, their minds tragically deteriorated from the effects of some dementing disease. What is the purpose of all that they are doing now if death is just the end of it all? But of course, death is not the end of it all, since one day each one of us is going to give account of our lives to our Creator. We all will die, yes, but we all will live for eternity, too, either in heaven (the renewed creation) with our Creator, or in hell, separated from Him for eternity.

As I thought about this, and again thought about Robert, the burden to warn the world about the true meaning of life and tell them the wonderful saving message of the gospel intensified. That's what Rob would want to happen. They need to care — they need to face the reality of death.

But what a difference when you know not only the reason as to why death is here — sin — but the fantastic news that the One who has power over death has already paid the penalty for sin, by dying on a cross and being raised from the dead.

It is my prayer that as a result of Rob's terrible disease, his message of spiritual healing will be used by the Lord to change the lives of countless people.

If you have never been "spiritually healed" and don't know the comfort of the Lord, I urge you to turn the pages, read the appendix, and act upon it.

After this manuscript was complete, Robert Mervyn Ham went to be with the Lord on June 9, 2002. This was the very same day that our father, seven years earlier, also passed into the same blessed surety of eternal life.

Here's the Good News

This book has sought, like all publications associated with *Answers in Genesis,* to give glory and honor to God as Creator. We are convinced of the truth of the biblical record of the real origin and history of the world and mankind.

Part of this real history is the bad news that the rebellion of the first man, Adam, against God's command brought death, suffering and separation from God into this world. We see the results all around us. All of Adam's descendants are sinful from conception (Ps. 51:5) and have themselves entered into this rebellion (sin). They therefore cannot live with a Holy God, but are condemned to separation from God. The Bible says that "all have sinned, and come short of the glory of God" (Rom. 3:23) and that all are therefore subject to "everlasting destruction from the presence of the Lord and from the glory of His power" (2 Thess. 1:9).

But the good news is that God has done something about it. "For God so loved the world, that He gave his only-begotten

Son, that whoever believes in Him should not perish, but have everlasting life" (John 3:16).

Jesus Christ the Creator, though totally sinless, suffered, on behalf of mankind, the penalty of mankind's sin, which is death and separation from God. He did this to satisfy the righteous demands of the holiness and justice of God, His Father. Jesus was the perfect sacrifice; He died on a cross, but on the third day He rose again, conquering death, so that all who truly believe in Him, repent of their sin and trust in Him (rather than their own merit), are able to come back to God and live for eternity with their Creator.

Therefore: "He who believes on Him is not condemned, but he who does not believe is condemned already, because he has not believed in the name of the only-begotten Son of God" (John 3:18).

What a wonderful Savior — and what a wonderful salvation in Christ our Creator! You can find out more about Jesus Christ, the Creator and Savior, by reading God's Word, the Bible, perhaps starting with John's gospel. Dear reader, if you have never known what it is to come to Christ for forgiveness of sin, and to have the assurance of eternal life, do it now before it is too late. Nothing else offers any hope, and nothing else makes sense of all of reality. Then find a local congregation of Christians who believe the Bible.

If you are having difficulty reconciling Bible/science issues, write to the nearest *Answers in Genesis* office, or check our website <www.AnswersInGenesis.org> for a wealth of information, resources, and encouragement. If you have become a Christian from reading this book, we would love you to write and tell us.

Answers in Genesis
P.O. Box 6330
Florence, KY 41022
USA

Answers in Genesis
P.O. Box 6302
Acacia Ridge DC
QLD 4110
Australia

Answers in Genesis
5-420 Erb St. West
Suite 213
Waterloo, Ontario
Canada N2L 6K6

Answers in Genesis
P.O. Box 3349
Durbanville 7551 Capetown
South Africa

Answers in Genesis
P.O. Box 39005
Howick, Auckland
New Zealand

Answers in Genesis
P.O. Box 5262
Leicester LE2 3XU
United Kingdom

Answers in Genesis
Attn: Nao Hanada
3317-23 Nagaoka, Ibaraki-machi
Higashi-ibaraki-gun, Ibaraki-
   ken 311-3116
Japan

In addition, you may contact:

Institute for Creation Research
P.O. Box 2667
El Cajon, CA 92021

Carl Wieland

A former Australian medical practitioner, Dr. Wieland is in great demand as a speaker on the scientific evidence for creation/flood, and its relevance to Christianity. Carl has written many books and articles on the subjects of creation, evolution, and Genesis.

Ken Ham

Ken Ham is one of the most in-demand Christian conference speakers in the United States. He is the executive director of Answers in Genesis and the author of many books emphasizing the relevance of the Book of Genesis.